In the Land of the Kami: A Journey into the Hearts of Japan

Michael Hoffman

"In The Land of the Kami: A Journey Into The Hearts of Japan." ISBN 978-1-62137-765-8 (softcover); 978-1-62137-766-5 (eBook).

Published 2015 by Virtualbookworm.com Publishing Inc., P.O. Box 9949, College Station, TX , 77842, US.

Author's Note

THE STORIES COLLECTED here were originally published between 2000 and 2013, all but three in the Sunday Time Out section of the Japan Times, the three exceptions being *Holy Fools*, *Death I Love You* and *Wet Sleeves*, which first appeared in a bimonthly magazine, now sadly defunct, called *The East*.

The topics treated are somewhat whimsical. This book would scarcely be justifiable otherwise – there are so many unwhimsical books on Japan, written by people whose qualifications are a lot more impressive than mine. The stories (most of them) arose not from what I knew and understood but from what I didn't know and wanted to understand: What *is* Zen? Who *was* Confucius, about whom we hear so much and know so little? What was it like to be a kid in Japan 10,000 years ago, or 1000, or 500? How did death come to seem, as it did for many centuries, so much more important to the Japanese than life?

I mentioned qualifications. I claim two. One is simply my presence here over many years, which has given me a familiarity with a country and a culture that remain and always will remain, familiarity notwithstanding, strange to me. Another is my ignorance – rather, my willing acknowledgment of my ignorance, the pride I seem to take in a quality others see as a problem, one to be solved with knowledge. Knowledge is good but, like everything else, only in moderation. Let knowledge inform ignorance, not stifle it. There are more questions in these stories than answers.

This is not, as will be clear by now, a work of scholarship. My debts to the historians, literary translators,

"Japanologists" who have been my teachers and guides on this journey are many and deep, gratefully acknowledged throughout the text.

Most Japanophiles love Japan for its present – its technology, its manga and anime, its safe streets and punctual trains. There's not much of that here. I love Japan for its past – not that I would have wanted to live in it, but contemplating it and the evidence it presents of the infinite mutability of human nature has been, and remains, an inexhaustible pleasure.

I drifted to Japan 33 years ago and, somewhat to my surprise, stayed. I sometimes wonder if I would have if not for Murasaki Shikibu and her majestic eleventh-century creation, the world's first novel, *The Tale of Genji*, owing nothing to Japan's cultural mentor, China, and antedating by a good half-millennium anything classifiable as a novel in the West. It was the first thing about Japan that astonished me.

Michael Hoffman
Hokkaido, Japan
August 2015

Table of Contents

Do Our Genitals
Define Us?

DO OUR GENITALS DEFINE US? Increasingly, they do not. Is sexuality more complicated than male/ female? Increasingly, it is.

Or maybe not "increasingly." Maybe the only thing that's changed over the ages is how much of our true selves society lets us show.

The Bible, keystone arch of Western civilization, had it all figured out. "Male and female created he them," says the Book of Genesis – "he" being God, "them" being us.

Turn now to Deuteronomy 22:5: "A woman must not wear men's clothing, nor a man wear women's clothing, for anyone who does so is an abomination to the Lord your God."

What would the Lord our God have made of the twenty-first century and its explosion of sexual alternatives? Same-sex marriage is the barest tip of the iceberg. Language strains to keep up with new practices, or old practices no longer cloaked in shame or social disapproval: cross-dressing, transgenderism, androgyny, hermaphroditism – and more, much more.

Japan, where same-sex marriage is hardly an issue, let alone a right, would offend the biblical God less than other places – which is ironic, because Japan is among the modern world's least Judeo-Christian counties.

1

Sexually, though – officially at least – it is overwhelmingly male/female.

Is officialdom deceived?

"Cool Japan" – manga- and anime-land – springs to mind as evidence that it is. Japan in fact was "cool" long before government PR machinery invented the label.

Myth takes us back to the formless void, where among the first generation of gods and goddesses are Izanagi ("He who invites") and Izanami ("She who invites"). The biblical God's creation of the universe is awesome and mysterious. Not so Izanagi and Izanami's begetting of Japan, charmingly narrated in the eighth-century chronicle *Nihon Shoki*.

Imagine sexually awakened gods who, like children, don't quite know what to do. They look at each other and are enchanted. Izanami speaks first: "What a splendid young man!" To which Izanagi replies, "What a splendid young woman!"

Their first offspring is a "leech child," born without limbs or bones. What had gone wrong? The older gods explained: Izanami, the female, had spoken first. Initiative was the male's prerogative. Chastened, they tried again. This time they got it right. Izanami gave birth to the islands of Japan, and to gods and goddesses without number. The poor deformed baby, placed in a boat of reeds, floated away, never to be heard of again.

Japan, begotten child of childlike gods, escaped the stern sexual discipline imposed by an asexual creator God whose grim intolerance of human passions caused him, for example, to destroy a city, Sodom, for a "sin" known ever since as sodomy. Japan acknowledged no sexual sins, least of all that one, as the sixteenth-century Christian missionaries who saw this "land of the gods" in its pristine state noted with squeamish disgust.

The missionaries were banished and Japan went into isolation for 250 years. In the mid-nineteenth century it was "opened." Powerless to resist American and European bullying, it feverishly set about "modernizing." Science and technology were not all it felt it had to learn from the West. Though it never turned Christian, it did adopt a quasi-Christian morality, toning down almost to the point of squelching the indigenous sexual playfulness (whose dark side, alas, is exploitation, of women in particular). The result was the buttoned-down Japan of the familiar stereotype – which, like all stereotypes, begs the proverbial grain of salt.

"Have you ever wondered how you look as a female?"

A man not predisposed to answer "yes" probably wouldn't be visiting a website that presumes to inquire. "Cross-dresser's paradise" – that's how the Elizabeth Club bills itself. Located in Tokyo's Asakusabashi district, it is one of hundreds of similar establishments whose existence on the fringes of conventional society suggests conventional society's failure to accommodate certain aspects – call them deviant if you like, but fewer and fewer people do – of human nature.

"Don't you want to become a lady of your dreams?" the website's enticement continues.

It's easy enough. "At Elizabeth, we want your feminine experience to be all you hoped for. There's a shop that carries everything you need to become a female: lingerie, stockings, wigs, high-heels, clothing, makeup goods, accessories, breast forms… After you change into women's clothes, our makeup artists, all young girls, will transform you to a girl or lady of your dream… There is no limit except for your imagination."

3

Clubs like this, and the widening appeal of cross-dressing and prime-time transgender TV stars – Matsuko Deluxe, Ai Haruna, Ikko – point to a restlessness within our conventional sexual boxes. Is it fanciful to foresee a time when we'll burst out of them altogether? If so, there's a lot of fanciful thinking around. Collectively it's called "postgenderism." One of its boldest exponents was feminist thinker Shulamith Firestone (1945-2012).

In *The Dialectics of Sex* (1970) she wrote, "The end goal of feminist revolution must be... not just the elimination of male privilege but of the sex distinction itself: genital differences between human beings would no longer matter culturally. The reproduction of the species by one sex for the benefit of the other would be replaced by artificial reproduction."

Male privilege four decades later remains alive and well, much more so in Japan than elsewhere, if the World Economic Form's oft-cited Global Gender Gap Reports are a fair measure. In 2012 Japan ranked 101st among 135 countries – in 2014 104th among 142 countries – in terms of female professional, economic and political empowerment.

Behind that is a long past that showed scant regard for women. Warriors despised their weakness; Buddhists dismissed them as polluted beings incapable of attaining Enlightenment; Confucianism stressed the obedience a wife owed her husband and a mother her son. The modernizing regime of the Meiji Era (1868-1912) assigned woman her post-Confucian place – no corporate warrior or captain of burgeoning industry, she, but a "good wife and wise mother" (*ryosai kenbo*); it was written into the Meiji Civil Code, which remained in effect until 1947.

Postgenderism? Not Japan's forté. Even the grand coming-out party that is Tokyo Rainbow Week, celebrated over ten heady days in April, of LGBT (lesbian, gay, bisexual, transgender) life, shows Japan to be rather behind most of the developed world, though slowly catching up. The gay pride movement in the United States goes back to 1968 (kindled, it is true, by a prevalent homophobia more virulent than anything Japanese LGBT people ever faced); Japan's did not begin until 1994.

All the same, there is a touch, sometimes more than a touch, of postgenderism in Japanese culture, going all the way back to Izanami and Izanagi's confusion over gender roles. Perhaps it's not quite what Firestone had in mind. Perhaps, though, it hints at a latent capacity, to be realized over time (for better or worse), for what she did have in mind. A whimsical notion, admittedly.

Let's see if it holds.

Manga and anime fans will know the term *futanari*, or "new half" – hermaphrodite characters endowed with feminine curves, voluptuous breasts and a virile penis.

Their popularity goes back to the 1990s and endures to this day. Possibly this has something to do with the economic downturn that started around then, eroding the socially sanctioned and officially promoted orthodoxies, sexual and otherwise, that had gone more or less unchallenged during the Meiji and postwar economic surges.

Possibly, too, there's a futanari element in the psychology of the nation itself.

American anthropologist Ruth Benedict (1887-1948) captured it in the title of her classic 1946 work on Japan, *The Chrysanthemum and the Sword* – beauty and strength, female and male. Among the book's

5

Japanese admirers was novelist Yukio Mishima (1925-1970). A year before his famous suicide by ritual samurai disembowelment and beheading, he made a speech in which, citing Benedict, he declared, "After the war the balance between these two (chrysanthemum and sword) was lost. The sword has been ignored since 1945. My ideal is to restore the balance. To revive the tradition of the samurai, through my literature and my action."

"The chrysanthemum and the sword" – they're in Japan's blood; both, together; at odds but inseparable. No man is *all* male, no woman *all* female. Femininity was despised in women – not in men. The fiercest warrior was likely to be something of a poet, shedding unashamed tears over the beauty of cherry blossoms and the dew on a flowering morning glory. Buddhism, the principal religion during the first thousand years of Japanese civilization, declared women to be unfit for Enlightenment – but not for reincarnation as a man in the next life. In some Buddhist sutras she changes her gender by meditating.

The female within the male, and the male within the female, seem closer to the surface in the Japanese tradition than in the standard Western ones. The 13th-century *Heike Monogatari*, an epic tale of the 12th-century Genpei civil war that marked the transition to military government under a succession of shoguns, tells of two brothers slain in battle and their widows who, to comfort their bereaved mother-in-law, present themselves to her clad in their late husbands' armor. This is a long way from the cross-dressing at the Elizabeth Club, but it had to start somewhere.

Some 450 years later, in 1686, the Osaka novelist Ihara Saikaku (1642-93) wrote *Gengobei, the Mountain of Love*, a cross-dressing tale whose most striking feature, besides the throbbing passion that animates it, is its perfect naturalness. Saikaku is evidently writing for readers who will be amused, and moved – but not shocked.

Gengobei is a young rake who "devoted himself to the love of young men. Not once in his life had he amused himself with the fragile, long-haired sex." When two of his especially beautiful lovers die suddenly, Gengobei enters the priesthood and renounces the world – not dreaming of the passion he has stirred in a pathetic young girl named Oman, "graced with such beauty that even the moon envied her." Who should she fall in love with but Gengobei, "who had never in his life given a thought to girls"?

Cutting her hair and dressing like a boy, Oman boldly sets out for Gengobei's mountain retreat. As a boy she is irresistible to him, but the truth is bound to out, and when it does, "'What difference does it make – the love of men or the love of women?' [Gengobei] cried, overpowered by the bestial passion which rules this fickle world."

By Saikaku's time, the theater known as kabuki was already a flourishing art form. Its roots lay in popular entertainments, circa 1600, on the dry bed of the Kamo River in Kyoto – singing, dancing, acrobatics, skits, burlesques. The earliest performers were female, some of them dressed as men.

Then came the *onnagata* – male players of female roles. They were Japan's first stars. The most famous of them all, Yoshizawa Ayame (1647-1709), was Saikaku's contemporary. No woman, it was said, was more womanly than he – neither onstage nor off, for though unambiguously male (he was married and the father of four sons) he lived his private life in women's clothes and with feminine speech mannerisms.

"Unless the onnagata lives as a woman in daily life," he wrote in a treatise considered to this day a handbook of the art, "he won't be an accomplished onnagata."

7

Yoshizawa set the feminine fashions of his day. Women learned from him, not he from them, how to dress, apply makeup and comport themselves for maximum coquettish effect.

So it was with his artistic descendants as well. "Why should women appear when I am here?" demanded Nakamura Utaemon V, a famed onnagata of the 1920s. "There is no woman in all Japan who acts as feminine as I do."

Two words often used today to sum up a progressive attitude towards sex are "tolerance" and "diversity." Human beings are not all of one sort; no one set of practices is "right," "good" or "natural" as against others that are "wrong," "evil" or "unnatural." A glance at the sexual frolics of premodern Japan might suggest precisely those qualities of tolerance and diversity.

Was Japan, before the West molded it in its own image, tolerant? One element it lacked might make it seem so – a "Lord your God" frowning on his creatures' "abominations."

"Sodomy" was an early casualty, the stigma remaining until the gay pride movement of our own time began to erode biblically-sanctioned homophobia. Japan, in that sense, was way ahead of its time.

In 1763 a satirical writer named Hiraga Gennai (1728-79) penned a gem of a story titled *Rootless Weeds*. His tale opens with Emma-O, the Buddhist lord of the underworld, about to pronounce judgment on a young monk who has just died of love for the onnagata Segawa Kikunojo II (a real-life actor who died in 1773). Counsel for the dead monk's defense pleads for leniency: "How about letting him off with a soak in a boiling cauldron?"

"Most definitely not!" thunders Emma-O. "I'm told that something called 'male homosexuality' can be found all across the human world, and I absolutely cannot allow that kind of thing."

To make a long story all too short, defense counsel produces a portrait of the onnagata – with whom Emma-O (did counsel foresee this?) promptly falls head over heels in love. What an unholy predicament!

"I hereby resign," declares Emma-O, "as supreme ruler of the underworld. What's a precious throne worth when I can go to the human world and share a pillow with *him*?"

Homosexuality in Japan "did not mean delicacy and effeminacy," writes historian Hiroshi Watanabe in *A History of Japanese Political Thought: 1600-1901*. "Quite the contrary. From the Tokugawa Period (1603-1867) into the Meiji years (1868-1912), to say of a man that he 'disliked women' was to express a certain amount of approbation... For many samurai, excessive contact with women ran the risk of diluting their masculinity, notwithstanding that heterosexual sex was essential to the continuity of the house. To work at winning the heart of a woman was even more demeaning."

Buddhist monks had other reasons for avoiding women. Religious celibacy vows do not seem to have precluded boys, however. "Boys appear to have served as surrogates for the females absent from the lives of the monks," writes historian Gary Leupp in *Male Colors: The Construction of Homosexuality in Tokugawa Japan*. "Various Tokugawa Period jokes indicate the conflation of boys and women, and of the anus and vagina, in monastic society. In one, a priest on a religious retreat asks a friend to make him an *onyake* (artificial leather anus) for use in lieu of a boy. But he adds the request that it taste like a vagina."

9

This is homosexuality not as lifestyle choice but as faute de mieux. Senior monks took under their wing acolytes young enough to look feminine, sexual relations being accepted as part of the acolytes' education. The boys were called *chigo*.

"Some monks during the medieval period," writes Leupp, "shaved [their chigos'] eyebrows, powdered their faces [and] dressed them in female garb."

One tradition has Minamoto Yoshitsune, a hero of the twelfth-century Genpei civil war, spending his early years as the chigo lover of an abbot. "During this period," writes Leupp, "[Yoshitsune] wears cosmetics, wears his hair up in a girlish bun, blackens his teeth [as women of the day did], and thinly pencils in lines over his shaven eyebrows."

Is this tolerance, or exploitation? It can be a fine line between the two, and though it's hard to enter into the feelings of people of bygone times, it's the persistent hint of exploitation that disqualifies premodern Japan, sexually liberated though it seems in some ways, as a model for our own sexual liberation today. If liberation for some means slavery for others, it's damaged goods. Women in particular have little reason to regret the passing of the past. "A wife must think of her husband as her lord and look up to him with humility," explains the *Onna no Daigaku (The Greater Learning for Women)*, a manual for female conduct written in the early 1700s. "A woman regards her husband as heaven."

Custom was custom, force was force. Most women submitted, with varying degrees of willingness, resignation and despair. Some did not submit. The mid-nineteenth century gives us the example of Matsuo Taseko (1811-94), an obscure peasant poetess from a village in present-day Niigata Prefecture who, in the 1850s and '60s, embraced the radical Imperial cause against the Tokugawa Shogun who had shown himself helpless against the intrusive foreigner.

The year 1862 found her in Kyoto among swordsmen, assassins, poets and rabble-rousers, all bent on overthrowing the shogun and "restoring" the Emperor to real, not merely ceremonial, power. These were the birth pangs of the Meiji Restoration of 1868.

What was Taseko doing in the thick of this maelstrom? The only violence that she herself perpetrated was in her vituperative anti-Tokugawa poetry. More startling than her presence was her husband's absence. "No other woman abandoned husband and family for the chaotic conditions in the capital [Kyoto]," notes her biographer, Anne Walthall, in *The Weak Body of a Useless Woman*.

Japanese history is rich in women of indomitable courage: a wife fighting and dying at her husband's side, a widow defending to the death her husband's name and cause. Taseko acted alone. Her husband, a well-to-do peasant, stayed home and minded the farm.

"Taseko," explains Walthall, "became androgynous, an *onna masurao* (a 'manly woman')... By appearing in [Kyoto] at this critical juncture, she usurped the male prerogative to move about and to act on one's own... not for her was the role usually assigned to women in revolution, that of 'giving moral support to their men folk.'"

In becoming an onna masurao, did Taseko sacrifice her gender, or free herself from it? One of her poems suggests that the sacrifice, if such indeed it was, meant little to her:

> How awful to have the
> ardent heart of a manly man
>
> and the useless body
> of a weak woman.

Postgenderism. When Taseko's femaleness hindered her, she shucked it. And women today? Among *shojo manga* (comics for young girls), none has ever matched the inexhaustible popularity of *Berusaiyu no Bara (The Rose of Versailles)*, which, since its original run in 1972-73, has been repeatedly recast as anime, films and musicals – all smash hits.

The story, set during the French Revolution, is about one Oscar Francois de Jariayes, born a girl but raised as a boy by a father who wanted a son. As a boy she masters fencing, horsemanship and combat; as a man she flings herself into the revolutionary drama and falls in love with a man. The all-female Takarazuka Revue has performed it over the years to audiences totaling millions. Its starring role, that of Lady Oscar, is a sure vehicle to superstardom for the lucky *otokoyaku* (female player of male characters – Takarazuka's answer to kabuki's onnagata) assigned to play it.

How to account for popularity on this scale? Evidently, today's young women see the sexually ambiguous Lady Oscar as a kind of role model. What does she say to them? That a female gets nowhere in the world as a mere woman? That any single gender – female *or* male – falls short of being fully human? That both genders are equally meaningless, relics of an outgrown stage in the evolution of our species?

Men, in that case, seem to be traveling the same road. Post-gender male par excellence is the *otaku*, the hyper-computerized "nerd" whose absorption in manga, anime and computer games renders him unfit for, uninterested in, and contentedly detached from, anything previous generations have recognized as "real life."

Her we are in the heart of "Cool Japan." In October 2008 a young man named Taichi Takashita circulated an online petition demanding the legal right to marry an anime character. "Nowadays," the petition explained, "we have no interest in the three-dimensional world. If it were possible, we would rather live in a two-dimensional world."

The desire to escape into a fantasy world is not new. What may be is the possibility of actually doing so – permanently. The 2-D girl of Takashita's dreams is Mikuru Asahina, a beautiful but shy time traveler who figures in an anime series titled *Haruhi Suzumiya* – concerning which there is this interesting sidelight: In 2010, it hit the electronic grapevine that Aya Hirano, the 22-year-old voice actress who voices the series' eponymous heroine, was not a virgin. The indignation and sense of betrayal that swept otakuland! One 23-year-old male fan told the weekly *Spa!* magazine at the time, "An idol must embody men's ideal. To otaku, virginity is an ideal."

Takashita may never win the legal right to marry Mikuru (though his petition drew three thousand signatures within two months), but he – like everyone else, nowadays – commands the technology to spend as much time with her as he pleases. Isn't that as good as legal marriage? It is, if "postgenderism" takes on the added meaning, as it seems to be doing, of "postsex."

(2013)

13

Jomon Venus

THIS STORY SPANS TEN THOUSAND YEARS, yet presents few recognizable individuals. Here's one:

"The earliest known Jomon man," writes J. Edward Kidder in *The Cambridge History of Japan*, "was uncovered in 1949 below a shell layer in the Hirasaka shell mound in Yokohama City. He stood rather tall for a Jomon person: about 163 cm... X-rays of his bones show growth interruptions, interpreted as near-fatal spells of extreme malnutrition during childhood. The joints testify to early aging. Virtually unused wisdom teeth are partial evidence of a life-expectancy of about thirty years.

He lived sometime between 7500 and 5000 BC, when Japan's population was probably around 22,000.

Jomon culture was not new even then. Its defining innovation, pottery, was already thousands of years old. It goes back to circa 10,500 BC. It is the oldest pottery in the world, most authorities agree. A sister art was the crafting of clay *dogu* (figurines), some twenty thousand of which have been reconstructed, shard by shard. A great many depict pregnant women, and they radiate a primitive, sometimes almost grotesque beauty whose impact, on first viewing, is positively startling.

Jomon life was certainly short, arguably nasty – but not brutish. The Jomon people's pottery, their figurines and what little remains of their bones all tell the same tale – in dim outline, to be sure – of primeval terror soothed by primeval joy; of savagery softened by kindliness; of an unremitting consciousness of death that somehow became life-affirming.

Rising seas were the prologue to Jomon's emergence, as they were to Japan's.

About twenty thousand years ago, stirred by a period of cyclical global warming, oceans submerged parts of northeast Asia and made islands of the continent's rim – "creating," in Kidder's words, "an environment in which a distinct insular culture began to take shape."

"Insular" is the feature that first sets Jomon apart – starkly – from its roots in the vast Siberian tundra. Nomad hunters pursuing big game found themselves trapped on islands in the making, where the giant beasts – mammoth, bison, rhinoceros, north Asian horses, Naumann elephants – died out as the climate warmed and foraging territory shrank. Smaller animals took their place – boar, raccoon dogs, hares, badgers. Succeeding millennia saw these new islanders relying less and less on hunting, more and more on fishing and gathering. Gathering especially.

Gathering stimulates, and is stimulated by, pottery. Pottery is a revolutionary technology. It permits storage, and the boiling of otherwise inedible plants. It fosters settlement. "Jomon people," writes archaeologist Richard Pearson in the International Jomon Culture Conference Newsletter, "achieved residential stability by a very early date, in comparison with other parts of the world. Villages of up to fifty people containing pit-house dwellings and storage pits date as early as 900 BC.

Nature, or the spirits, were kind to them. "It appears," says Pearson, "that the [Jomon] had a wide

16

variety of plant foods available to them in comparison with the peoples of Europe and the Near East who lived in colder and drier conditions."

Their very success as hunters, fishers and gatherers – archaeologists count some six hundred types of Jomon food, including a "Jomon bread" made from eight different kinds of wild bean skins – helps explain their failure (or disinclination) to develop agriculture beyond very occasional, very tentative experiments.

"Jomon's existence in Japan for almost ten thousand years," note Kiyoshi Yamaura and Hiroshi Ushiro in the Smithsonian publication *Ainu: Spirit of a Northern People*, "makes it one of the longest-running single traditions in the world, whose hunting-and-gathering economy was so well adapted to the environmental conditions that few economic disruptions seem to have occurred."

Generally classed as Neolithic (New Stone Age) on account of their polished stone tools and pottery, Jomon people somehow resisted the typical Neolithic evolution from gathering to cultivating. Whole civilizations had risen, fallen and risen again before Japanese earth was first broken, circa 300 BC, by the iron spade. Resistance endured longest on the northernmost island of Hokkaido, where the Ainu, linked by ethnologists to Jomon man with disputed degrees of consanguinity, maintained a hunting-gathering culture well into the nineteenth century.

Japan's first farmers were Jomon's eventual supplanters – mainland immigrants known today as the Yayoi. They too were Neolithic, at least at first, but of a more progressive, more austere stamp. They brought with them another innovation apparently unknown to Jomon man: war.

17

The oldest recognizable Jomon site is at Hanawadai in present-day Ibaraki Prefecture. It dates back to what is classified, somewhat misleadingly, as Earliest Jomon (circa 7500-5000 BC; the label was already in place when new discoveries compelled recognition of a Sub-earliest or "Incipient" Jomon period, which lasted some five thousand years).

The Hanawadai site consists of five house pits about ten meters apart. None contained a fireplace; warming and cooking fires were set outdoors. "The little band of occupants," writes Kidder, "could hardly have numbered more than ten or fifteen."

The ensuing millennia wrought change, but the pace was glacial. There was no "Jomon Revolution." Neither agriculture nor metal came to disturb the peace or expand the horizons. An Earliest Jomon man returning to life four thousand years later – roughly the time span separating us from Abraham's departure for the Promised Land – would have found things pretty much as he had left them.

Some progress he would have noticed. Fireplaces had moved indoors. The pit dwellings that had housed Jomon man from the beginning were sturdier and more sheltering. Villages were larger, trade networks broader. Fish hooks and harpoons were now suitable for deep-sea fishing in dugout canoes six meters long. Bows were firmer, poisoned hunting arrows deadlier. Food was better and more varied, and life was somewhat easier. "Softer foods and improved tools," writes Kidder of around 3000 BC, "spared teeth from the inordinate wear experienced by their ancestors."

Still, and despite a ten-fold-plus rise in population (to 250,000), over those four thousand years, individual life expectancy remained unaltered: fifteen years at birth, thirty in the unlikely event you survived childhood. A site in Aomori Prefecture has yielded burial jars for more than 880 infants – six times the number of adults. Fertility and death walked hand in hand.

The name "Jomon" means "cord-marked," and describes a decorative flourish that adorned the earliest Jomon pottery – and the latest, representing an artistic continuity of ten thousand years.

That common trait aside, Jomon pottery presents a dazzling variety of shapes, surface treatment and artistic motifs. "It roams into lavish conceptions of form and decorations probably unsurpassed in any time or place," enthused Scottish archaeologist Neil Munro in *Prehistoric Japan* (1908).

You have to remind yourself, as you admire it, that the technology involved was almost inconceivably primitive. Each article was shaped by hand and hardened in outdoor bonfires. The potter's wheel and the kiln were undreamed of. In use in Mesopotamia as early as 3500 BC, they took thousands of years to reach Japan. Their use is one of the features that sets Yayoi apart from Jomon.

How the leap came to be made from pots, jars, lamps and burial urns to human figures is anyone's guess.

Containers are common to Neolithic cultures; ceramic sculpture is not, and Jomon's, affirms Naoaki Ishikawa, chief curator of the Otaru Museum in Hokkaido, is likely the oldest of its kind in the world

The earliest pieces are some twelve thousand years old, comparable in antiquity to the Cro-Magnon cave art of France and Spain. Cro-Magnon artists painted Ice Age animals – hunters' prey – on cave walls. The Jomon sculpted women, most of them visibly pregnant.

19

Japan's oldest known dogu figurine, 5.8 cm tall, consists of a lump of clay representing a head mounted neckless on a lump of clay representing a torso, with only the swelling breasts to put the object in perspective and suggest a significance. It was unearthed at a Sub-earliest Jomon site in Mie Prefecture. Thousands of years pass with much production but little progress, and then, more or less suddenly, there is a change. By 3500 BC we discern a heightened awareness of the face and its peculiar nuances. Eyes, nose and mouth, the latter generally open – to convey what? – are apparently no longer beside the point. There is an urgency reflected in some of those faces: they seem almost to be trying to tell us something, and to be distressed at our inability to understand.

Centuries pass; the faces grow more lifelike but less human. One looks strikingly like a cat. Another is oddly reminiscent of a Buddhist bodhisattva, her head rising to a domelike protuberance, her palms joined as though in prayer. She is crouching – one of a number in that posture; the posture of childbirth, scholars conjecture.

One figure, unearthed in Nagano Prefecture and dating from the Middle Jomon period (circa 3500-2400 BC), is famous as the so-called Jomon Venus. Her swollen belly and ample hips are in odd contrast to her rather perfunctory breasts. She is fertility personified; her heart-shaped face, with its empty eyes and half-open mouth, seems unequal to expressing the mystery of it all. She stands 27 cm tall, making her rather large (the largest dogu of all is 45 cm tall and seems to be wearing flared trousers). Venus' hair is most elaborately coiffed, a fitting home for the lacquered combs found in profusion at Jomon sites everywhere.

Roughly contemporary with Venus, dug up in Tokyo, is a stunning creation. A mother (her head, alas, lost) sits cradling an infant, her breasts hovering protectively over the child. The mood is deeply tender. This is rare. Fertility is the theme common to all Jomon art – and yet, writes Kunihiko Fujinuma in *Jomon no Dogu* (Jomon Clay Figurines), "although there are many dogu of women with swollen bellies, of mother and child together only two have been found."

Latest of all, towards Jomon's close beginning around 1000 BC, the faces grow increasingly strange, as if realistic portraiture, so laboriously achieved, has at last been cast aside as something outgrown. Eyes are large circles. They are more like goggles than eyes.

What does it all mean?

Hypotheses abound – and will have to suffice, in the absence of certainties. Physical remains make us want to, goad us to try to, but hardly render us able to penetrate even the surface thoughts of a people so remote from us. "We must never forget," writes Takura Izumi in *Jomon Doki Shutsugen* (The Advent of Jomon Pottery), "that modern man," accustomed to manipulating nature through agriculture and the other civilized arts, "cannot possibly grasp the intimate feelings of people who lived by hunting and gathering."

The potters and artists of Jomon were probably women. Men's work was hunting and fishing. Women did everything else, including the most important thing of all – bringing forth new life.

Did the dogu, even the more realistic ones, depict living women? Do their tattoo-like markings, their hair styles, their facial expressions and body proportions, help us visualize the Stone Age inhabitants of Japan as they really were? Or were they idealized beings, spirits? Either way, they were evidently objects of reverence.

21

A late nineteenth-century conjecture had it that their purpose was to cure illness or injury; the figure would have been made in the likeness of the sufferer and broken, to drive the evil spirit away. Broken they certainly are, as modern archaeologists find them – but is the breakage the work of time or of Jomon shamans? Some experts say the one, some the other.

The notion foundered on other grounds. For example, there are almost no male dogu. Did only women get sick? Only pregnant women?

And if the figurines were curative, why did their production die out with Jomon? Why are there no Yayoi dogu?

Could it be that, radiant with meaning to hunter-gatherers living in groups too loosely organized to be called governed societies, the dogu were irrelevant to Yayoi cultivators ruled by chieftains or (as a contemporary Chinese chronicle styled them) "kings"?

"The Jomon world swarmed with spirits," writes Fujinuma. He does not use the word "gods." Spirits lack the identity or authority of gods. They are anarchic, amorphous, indefinable, perhaps even homeless. "Possibly," Fujinuma speculates, "a spirit would be pleased to lodge in a form that resembled itself" – and in so doing confer upon her devotees the one gift they craved, the gift on which life depended, the one thing that mattered – not wealth, not happiness, not comfort, not victory in battle, not longevity, but fertility – fertility in all its forms, human, animal and vegetal. An agricultural society can labor for fertility. Gatherers have no recourse but to pray for it. The female figurines of Jomon may best be seen as tangible prayers.

And they were effective. Japan was, by and large, kind to the Jomon. It fed them for ten thousand years without imposing on them the rigors of agriculture and government.

In return, there is a kindly strain in the Jomon that reflects the relative benignity of their environment. The potential savagery of the human heart in primitive conditions is limitless. Izumi records an ancient belief in southern China that a mother who ate the flesh of her firstborn would be especially fecund thereafter – and in fact, he writes, pottery has been found bearing traces of human infant bones mixed with fish bones. No comparable horror seems to have infected the Jomon.

Another scourge the Jomon apparently escaped, or shunned, is war. "Of the more than five thousand skeletons excavated from Jomon sites," writes historian William Wayne Farris in *Sacred Texts and Buried Treasures*, "only about ten give evidence of violent death." The corresponding figures for Yayoi, he says, are one thousand skeletons and more than one hundred violent deaths.

(2008)

In the Land of the Kami

"In some rural areas even today, elderly villagers face the rising sun each morning, clap their hands together, and hail the appearance of the sun over the peaks of the nearby mountain as 'the coming of the kami."

– Historian Takeshi Matsumae, 1993

WHAT IS SHINTO? There is no answer; its devotees hardly seek one.

Who, or what, are the *kami*, the myriad objects of Shinto worship? Nobody knows; knowledge seems beside the point.

"The Japanese people themselves do not have a clear idea regarding the kami," writes Sokyo Ono in *Shinto: The Kami Way* (1962). "They are aware of the kami intuitively at the depth of their consciousness and communicate with the kami without having formed the kami-idea conceptually or theologically."

Ambiguity is fertile breeding ground, and kami, whatever they are – gods? spirits? natural? supernatural? good? evil? both? neither? – crop up everywhere, in overwhelming profusion, in every conceivable form. A tenth-century text enumerates 3132 of them – the upper crust, so to speak. It's a far from exhaustive list.

Most kami are purely local; many are ancestral; many more are animals – tigers, wolves, hares, serpents;

or natural phenomena – wind, rain, thunder ("the kami that rumbles"); or natural objects – most famously Mount Fuji, "the mysterious kami" of the poets.

A numberless horde are Japan's kami. The *Nihon Shoki*, an eighth-century court compendium of myth and tendentious history, speaks of "kami that shone with a luster like fireflies, and evil kami that buzzed like flies."

"God" or "deity" seems the best the English language can do with "kami," but this misleads by suggesting a level of exaltation foreign to Japanese worship. The Emperor's former status as a "living God" was not what many horrified Westerners took it to be. In fact, he was a "manifest kami" – hardly the same thing and much less shocking.

Anything, or anyone, can become a kami by being striking or, in some undefined way, "superior" – the literal meaning of the word. The classic definition comes from the eighteenth-century nativist thinker Motoori Norinaga, who dedicated his life to exalting supra-rational Japanese purity over Buddhism's and Confucianism's corrupt enslavement, as he saw it, to human reason.

"I do not yet understand the meaning of the term 'kami'," wrote Norinaga in *The Spirit of the Gods* (1771). "It is hardly necessary to say that it includes human beings. It also includes such objects as birds, beasts, trees, plants, seas, mountains and so forth. In ancient usage, anything whatsoever which was outside the ordinary, which possessed superior power or which was awe-inspiring, was called kami... Evil and mysterious things, if they are extraordinary and dreadful, are called kami..."

Rooted in the spontaneous nature-worship of deep prehistory, Shinto is probably the most archaic living religion anywhere in the developed world.

Why is it living? How did it survive?

The greatest challenge Shinto encountered came not from modern times but from Buddhism.

It's a story that goes back some fifteen hundred years. Indian in origin and newly arrived in Japan via China and Korea, Buddhism was everything Shinto was not – elegant, systematic, moral, philosophical, profound. No two world views could have been more different.

Preliminary skirmishes flared into civil war. The Buddhist faction won. That was in A.D. 587. Around the same time, in far distant lands utterly unknown to the actors in the Japanese drama, Roman Christianity was confronting the heathen religions of Dark Age Europe. Heathenism died out. Shinto did not. Why?

Possibly its very nebulousness saved it.

Shinto defies a direct approach. It is easier to say what it is not than what it is; easier to say what it lacks than what it has.

In its pristine form – as distinct from what the state and scholars like Norinaga made of it from time to time – it has no gods more exalted than kami, no myths that rise above childishness, no charismatic founder, no sacred texts, no art, scarcely any notion of good and evil, no morals, no ethics, no punishment, no concept of personal responsibility, of the soul, of immortality.

There's no human or animal sacrifice either, inseparable though these expressions of cosmic terror generally are from mankind's dawning religious consciousness.

Is it even a religion? Ono, a noted Shintoist scholar, calls it "more than a religious faith," but you could just as easily call it less than one. "It is an amalgam," says Ono, "of attitudes, ideas, and ways of doing things that through two millennia and more have become an integral part of the way of the Japanese people."

It was in the air Japan breathed. It never even had a name until Buddhism came along and forced it to think of itself as something nameable. *Butsudo*, the Way of the Buddha, suggested *Shinto*, the Way of the Kami.

Shinto is blessed with a joyously exuberant view of the world. It has no heaven because it doesn't need one. "This world," writes Ono, "is inherently good."

There is evil, certainly, but it is ascribed either to pollution, which can be purified, or to an intrusion from other worlds, which can be exorcised. Pollution arises from contact with illness, blood, death. Childbirth is deemed more polluting than murder if the murderer spills no blood.

Ono offers this peculiar explanation: "The Shinto manner of grasping truth takes into consideration the fact that values are constantly changing. For example, in Shinto ethics nothing – sex, wealth, killing, etc. – is regarded as unconditionally evil."

Norinaga, the eighteenth-century nativist, in effect transmutes evil into good by making it no less divine: "Among the kami there are good and bad ones. Their actions are in accordance with their different natures, so they cannot be understood by ordinary reason... In foreign countries all the good and bad things that happen are either attributed to karmic retribution according to the Way of the Buddha or else thought to be, according to the various Ways of China, acts of heaven... All these theories are mistaken... It is entirely due to the will of the kami that there is harm in the world, that everything cannot be proper and in accord with reason, and that there are wicked things."

Buddhism, when at last it put down inextricable roots in Japanese society, must have seemed to the Shinto mind a bitter if intellectually bracing pill.

"As opposed to Shinto, which views physical life as basically good and acceptable," writes H.E. Plutschow in *Chaos and Cosmos* (1990), "Buddhism regards life as suffering, and physical existence as basically undesirable."

Are these contrary outlooks reconcilable? Astonishingly, mysteriously, they turned out to be.

Shinto's roots reach so deeply into the past as to be scarcely traceable. Before agriculture, before metal, the Stone Age hunter-gatherers of the long Jomon Period (c.10,500 BC – c.300 BC), in their instinctive veneration of mountains, fields and streams, were in a sense proto-Shintoists.

The wet-rice cultivators of the succeeding Yayoi Period (c.300 BC – A.D. 300) worshipped a rice spirit "believed to dwell at harvest time in specially reaped sheaves of rice," writes Matsumae, the historian. "These sheaves were enshrined in grain storehouses" – apparent archetypes of the distinctive and rudely beautiful Shinto shrine architecture we know today.

Sun worship too, subsequently to loom so large in the official, militarist "state Shinto" of the twentieth century, is a Yayoi legacy. The famous mythological quarrel between the benign sun goddess, Amaterasu, and her raging brother, the storm god Susano'o, who desecrated her rice fields, reflects the fearfully precarious footing on which Yayoi agriculture stood.

Its long prehistory over at last, Japan enters recorded history as the kingdom of Yamato (c. A.D. 250-587), its kings (or emperors) increasingly acknowledged by rival clan chiefs as supreme. That this supremacy was largely religious was of great significance for the future of kami worship. So far, cultic evolution had been slow and natural. Now it would be rapid and political.

Imperial ascendency came to rest on divine descent. Benevolent and charming in the early myths, Amaterasu, emerging in the sixth century as the Imperial ancestress, grew ominously, though fleetingly, awesome. Buddhism in the next century tamed her; Confucianism, a later import, dimmed her. For centuries, even as folk Shinto, or "shrine Shinto," flourished in villages and urban plebian quarters, Amaterasu herself eked out a bare survival as "avatar" of the Roshana Buddha.

But her transient brilliance inspired scattered minds here and there – Norinaga's, for instance. In the fullness of time it resurged.

Apostle of the past and unconscious herald of the future, Norinaga in 1771 wrote: "[The Sun Goddess] is without peer in the whole universe, casting her light to the very ends of heaven and earth and for all time. There is not a single country in the world which does not receive her beneficent illuminations... This goddess is the splendor of all splendors. However, foreign countries, having lost the ancient traditions of the Divine Age, do not know the meaning of revering this goddess."

They were, of course, to learn, though Norinaga in his own day seemed more wistful than prophetic. Long relegated to an official netherworld, Shinto under the 1868 Meiji Imperial Restoration was abruptly adopted as the state cult. Shinto myths, taught in schools as historical fact, propelled Japan first into the most intensive modernization the world had ever seen, then headlong into the most destructive war the world has ever known.

The curtain came down on state Shinto in 1945, its abolition decreed under the Occupation by the Supreme Commander for the Allied Powers – "in order," reads a SCAP memorandum to the Japanese government, "to prevent the recurrence of the perversion of Shinto theory and beliefs into militaristic and ultranationalistic propaganda designed to delude the Japanese people and lead them into wars of aggression."

There remains to this day shrine Shinto – unperverted Shinto, we might call it – at the heart of which are Japan's ongoing wealth of timeless festivals – timeless in two senses of the word: timelessly ancient, timelessly eternal.

Dancing and carousing celebrants welcoming, entertaining and finally seeing off local kami in due season perform rites as old as mankind. Shinto festivals, each distinctively local and yet all so essentially alike that some scholars infer an ancient proto-festival from which they all descend, represent order destroyed, disorder tamed, order restored.

On this ritual representation depend cosmic order, always precarious, and kami benevolence, never to be taken for granted.

(2010)

Ten Thousand Years of Childhood

CHILDHOOD. WE ALL KNOW IT, we've all been through it, we've all lost it. Memory retains traces of it. We recall facts, incidents, fragments – but not what it *feels* like to be a child. Childish feelings are nameable to the adult, but not recoverable. They are on the other side of an impassable boundary between the adult's world and the child's.

As with individuals, so with nations. History, made by grownups and written by grownups, forgets its children. We scour the history books in vain, mostly, for the children of the past. The historical drama as it comes down to us has few child actors.

Let us therefore, drawing on archaeology and literature where history fails us, welcome the children of old Japan back onstage.

It's a long story, thousands upon thousands of years long – with a strange trajectory: from fertility and mortality, twin preoccupations of prehistory, to infertility and longevity, characteristic idiosyncrasies of our own day.

Japan's current birth rate hovers around 1.3 children per woman, the world's second lowest after Hong Kong's.

Its population has been in decline since 2005. Challenging careers, the high cost of child rearing, the attractions of freedom and a skewed social system that places an inordinate domestic burden on women are all reasons not to have children. Pets seem to be replacing them. The nation's 23.2 million dogs and cats far outnumber its 17 million children under sixteen.

What would women of the Stone Age Jomon Period (circa 10,500–300 BC) have thought of that? Jomon ceramic sculpture, among the world's oldest, has one overriding motif – pregnancy. Thousands of years before agriculture, before metal, before the potter's wheel and the potter's kiln, at the very dawn of human consciousness on these islands, birth, the bringing forth of new life, was uppermost in the mind.

So was its concomitant, death. Life expectancy at birth was fifteen years. It's eighty-two today. Few Jomon children survived infancy. A Jomon site in Aomori Prefecture has yielded burial jars for more than 880 infants – six times the number of adults. Massive fecundity was humanity's only lifeline. The first battle on the Japanese archipelago was fought against no human enemy but against extinction. It lasted thousands of years and was won – barely – by women having children, and children, the hardiest of them, clinging to life against unfathomable odds.

It's not easy being a child in Japan. Proof is a finding that nearly a quarter of all Japanese junior high school children suffer from latent if not full-blown depression.

The scale is new; the phenomenon not. It goes back at least a thousand years, as a tenth-century diary by a

Kyoto noblewoman establishes beyond doubt. The diary is titled *Kagero Nikki (The Gossamer Years)*. The author's name is unknown, but her plight is famous. Unhappily married to a prince with eight wives vying for his whimsical attention (polygamy was the norm among the aristocrats of the time), she takes a perverse pleasure in her sorrow and her tearful rage. To her only son she is, after her fashion, a devoted mother – but as any offspring of a twentieth- or twenty-first-century broken home can attest, the child never comes off unscathed.

"The boy" – the diary doesn't name him – was born in 955. The marriage, never happy, was by then already breaking down, and the author's sardonic comment as the boy turns three is a gem of compressed pathos: "The child, who was beginning to talk, took to imitating the words with which his father always left the house: 'I'll come again soon, I'll come again soon,' he would chant, rather stumbling in the effort. I was sharply conscious of my loneliness as I listened to him. My nights too were lonely…"

"One day" – the boy is ten or eleven at the time of this entry – "when [the prince and I] had been taking our ease rather pleasantly together, a series of trivialities led to strong words on both sides, and he left in a fit of rage. Calling our son out to the veranda, he announced that he did not intend to come again. The boy came back into the room weeping bitterly. He refused to answer my questions…"

The years pass. The boy is fifteen, the prince his usual insouciant, neglectful self. "I was obsessed," writes the author, "with thoughts of death and suicide, but concern for the boy restrained me… Once, to see how he would react, I suggested to the boy that I might retire and become a nun. Child though he was, he burst into tears. 'If you do that, I will become a priest,' he said. 'What reason would there be for me to go on as I am?'"

The following year, mother and son retreat for spiritual solace to a mountain temple: "I had come here by my own choice, and I was content. I could not help brooding nonetheless over the load of karma that had driven me to such a hermitage. Also I was distressed that the boy seemed so apathetic… All day long he stayed shut up in the house, and as I watched him try unsuccessfully to get down the rough food to which I had condemned us – it was all right for me, this eating of pine needles, but what of him? – I would feel the tears welling up."

All this portends a hopelessly neurotic future for the boy. He seems, however, to escape the worst. The diary breaks off abruptly in 974. The boy is nineteen. Having secured an Imperial Palace appointment as "Vice-Chief of the Right Horse Stables," he is courting a certain lady via shy exchanges of poems, some of which his mother, a noted poetess, helps write.

Nineteen was late for a first courtship. The eponymous hero of Murasaki Shikibu's eleventh-century novel *The Tale of Genji* was married at twelve, immediately following his coming-of-age ceremony. "The nuptial observances were conducted with great solemnity. The groom seemed… quite charming in his boyishness. The bride [aged sixteen] was… somewhat ill at ease with such a young husband."

Well she might be. She would have been more so had she divined Genji's own feelings, compounded of yearning for his late mother and longing for his royal father's new sixteen-year-old consort, chosen as such for her striking resemblance to the dead lady.

But the emotions of the child-betrothed were beside the point, trumped by political considerations quite beyond their grasp. "Marriage politics" sounds better than war as a means of securing power, but it was hard on the children.

Masters of the art were the Fujiwara clan, the power behind the throne throughout the peaceful and unwarlike Heian Period (794-1185). The point was to marry Fujiwara daughters into the Imperial Family – to a cadet like Genji or, better still, to a child-Emperor. Most Emperors of the time were children, starting with eight-year-old Emperor Seiwa in 858. Emperor Ichijo was six when he ascended the throne in 980, and ten when married to a fifteen-year-old Fujiwara cousin – whose father acted as regent. The Emperor's sole political function was to produce a Fujiwara-related heir, in favor of whom, under Fujiwara pressure, he would abdicate just as he was growing old enough to exercise independent judgment – at twenty-six in Seiwa's case, thirty in Ichijo's.

Few early cultures can boast four hundred years of peace. It is one of Heian Japan's claims to fame. Courtiers in Kyoto, the capital, were too absorbed in their poetry, music, perfume-blending, wine-bibbing and amorous intrigues to notice the martial spirit brewing offstage in the remote eastern wilds near today's Tokyo. The inevitable eruption caught them unawares; their refined, exclusive little society sank like a stone.

The issue was an Imperial succession dispute that gave two rival military clans, the Heike and the Minamoto, a pretext to assert themselves.

The Heike's initial ascendency began to crumble around 1180. The resurgent Minamoto overran the capital and pursued the retreating Heike south. Emperor at the time was Antoku, age eight. With him in tow, the Heike took to their ships – prelude to the famous naval battle at Dannoura, fought in the strait between Honshu and Kyushu.

The Heike cause was hopeless. The thirteenth-century epic *Heike Monogatari* chronicles the agony of defeat. A Heike court lady, "taking the Emperor in her arms, spoke thus: 'Though I am but a woman I will not fall into the hands of the foe, but will accompany our Sovereign Lord.'

"With a look of surprise and anxiety on his face [the Emperor] inquired... 'Where is it that you are going to take me?'

"Turning to her youthful Sovereign with tears streaming down her cheeks, she answered: '... This land is... now but a vale of misery. There is a Pure Land of happiness beneath the waves, another capital where no sorrow is. Thither it is that I am taking our Lord.'

"And thus comforting him, she bound his long hair up in his dove-colored robe and... sank with him at last beneath the waves."

In 1971, the psychiatrist Takeo Doi published a landmark book later translated into English as *The Anatomy of Dependence*. It introduced the concept of *amae*, defined as "the craving of a newborn child for close contact with its mother, and, in the broader sense, the desire to deny the fact of separation that is an inevitable part of human existence." Healthy and natural in an infant, amae persisting into adulthood to the point of defining the culture implies something like mass pathology.

"I would suggest," Doi writes, "that the basic emotional urge that has fashioned the Japanese for two thousand years is none other than the amae mentality.

The realization that this mentality... is basically childish did not, I suspect, occur to anyone until after Japan's defeat in World War Two."

Something of the sort must have struck General Douglas MacArthur, who, during the postwar Occupation he headed as Supreme Commander of the Allied Powers, allegedly described Japan as "a nation of twelve-year-olds."

Charles Dunn, in his 1969 book *Everyday Life in Traditional Japan*, writes of the Edo Period (1603-1867), "In the lower classes at least, mothers breast-fed their children for as long as possible – much longer than in Europe – partly because they believed that they would not conceive again until the child was weaned and partly because they kept their babies near to them all the time. The baby was carried around on its mother's back... There it passed the day until bedtime... At night it shared its mother's bed, and even when a child grew big enough to require a bed of its own it would continue to sleep in the same room as its parents. The constant company of others probably had its effect in later life, when to be alone was felt to be most undesirable."

A late 1960s Asahi Shimbun poll of University of Tokyo students, cited by Doi, shows mothers topping the list of individuals the students most respected.

The paradox is plain to anyone familiar with the harsh martial ethos of much of Japan's history. Amae seems to fit Heian Japan and seems also to fit the unheroic mores of our own day, but the age of the samurai, born of the Minamoto-Heike war and surviving into the twentieth century, certainly showed a sterner face to the world.

Inazo Nitobe's English-language classic *Bushido* (1900) is no doubt a romanticized portrayal of the "Way of the warrior" by a nostalgic writer clinging to a vanishing past, but it confirms that, ideally at least, a samurai childhood was no wallow in amae.

"Stories of military exploits were repeated almost before boys left their mother's breast," Nitobe writes. "Does a little booby cry for any ache? The mother scolds him in this fashion: 'What a coward to cry for a trifling pain! What will you do when your arm is cut off in battle? What when you are called upon to commit hara-kiri?'

"Parents," he continues, "with sternness sometimes verging on cruelty, set their children tasks that called forth all the pluck that was in them... Occasional deprivation of food or exposure to cold was considered a highly efficacious test for inuring them to endurance... In days when decapitation was public, not only were small boys sent to witness the ghastly scene, but they were made to visit alone the [execution ground] in the darkness of night and there to leave a mark of their visit on the trunkless head."

Probably the most famous samurai child in Japanese history is Masatsura, son of a semi-legendary fourteenth-century swashbuckler named Kusunoki Masashige. The Kamakura shogunate founded by the Minamoto clan two centuries earlier was still in place but tottering. Long resentful of its subjection in all but name to the shogun, the Imperial court in Kyoto watched for its chance. Emperor Godaigo was the man to seize it. He was an adult, for one thing, not a child like most of his predecessors. And he was of a firm, unyielding character, determined to rule as well as reign.

Rallying to his cause was the obscure warrior Masashige. His forces were few but his ninja-style tactics were masterful. After many ups and downs they won the day. In 1333, Kamakura was captured. The Kamakura Period (1185-1333) was over.

But Godaigo's "Restoration" was short-lived. Key supporters soon turned against him. Only Masashige remained loyal. In 1336, vastly outnumbered, he faced . the rebels at the Battle of Minato River near today's Kobe. With him was ten-year-old Masatsura.

"The parting between Masashige and his son used to be included in all elementary school readers and was the subject of a patriotic song... prohibited by the Occupation authorities in 1945," notes historian Ivan Morris in *The Nobility of Failure* (1975).

Morris quotes the song: "Wiping away his tears, Masashige calls his son. 'Your father,' he says, 'is bound for Hyogo Bay, and there he will lay down his life. You, Masatsura, have come with me thus far, but now I bid you hurry home.'"

The boy's protests are overruled: "Go, Masatsura, back to our village, where your aging mother waits!" Reluctantly, he goes.

The battle was fought, the loyalists were defeated. Masashige, samurai that he was, disemboweled himself. His body was found, his head severed and exposed to public view. Then it was sent to his family.

The fourteenth-century epic *Taiheiki* takes up the story. Masatsura "gazed at his father's face which had been so completely transformed, and observed his mother's inconsolable sorrow." Determined to follow his father in death, Masatsura reaches for his sword. His mother stays him: "Though you have a child's mind, consider the matter carefully!" He must live, she admonishes him, to fight another day.

Persuaded, he spends the rest of his childhood developing his fighting powers. "He would knock down other boys," writes Morris, "and, while pretending that he was about to decapitate them, would shout, 'Thus do I take the head of an enemy of the Court!'"

In 1347, aged twenty-two, he led a loyalist uprising and committed ritual suicide when it was defeated.

After three centuries of civil wars, suddenly there was peace. Edo Period Japan, after 1603, didn't quite turn its swords into plowshares, but it did unite under a central government based in Edo (present-day Tokyo) and withdraw from almost all commerce with the outside world, submitting, at times grudgingly, to a kind of warrior's peace. Samurai remained samurai and as a military caste claimed special privileges, but they no longer fought.

The battlefield gave way to the pleasure quarters.

Nationwide there were twenty-four of these urban enclaves of officially tolerated prostitution – islands, in a rigidly controlled society, of healthy, ribald, mass, plebeian, exuberant sex.

That's one view – not the child's, of course, and the child's view is relevant because children inevitably were drawn into the life of the quarters. Many were sold into it. Some were accidentally born into it – relatively few, since abortion nipped most quarter pregnancies in the bud. Infanticide claimed most of the rest.

Crushing taxes, frequent crop failure and hopeless indebtedness were the average farmer's lot in Edo Japan. "Many," writes the historian Dunn, "were forced to sell their daughters into what amounted to slavery. The brothels and entertainment districts were provided with their women by this means... Although there was considerable distress in individual cases, there was no general condemnation of this practice, and in the atmosphere of the times it is probable that the majority of girls found their new way of life at least no worse than the one they were leaving."

The system had its defenders well into modern times, the quarters not being abolished until 1946. In 1896 Prime Minister Hirobumi Ito praised as Confucian filial piety the child-prostitute's "lofty desire to help her poor parents or relations."

So deep a sense of duty towards parents may well have arisen from a feeling of being lucky to be alive. Abortion and infanticide were "as much a part of the experience of pregnancy as childbirth itself," writes religious studies scholar William Lindsey in *Fertility and Pleasure* (2007).

Infanticide in particular, he says, was widespread enough to depress population growth for 150 years from the early 1700s – a bizarre throwback to the Jomon struggle to survive infancy and an uncanny precursor to today's scarcity of children. "The question of the child's fate, 'to be kept' or 'sent back,' was a standard query that a midwife posed after successfully accomplishing delivery."

Children belong in school. That is the modern view, more or less unquestioned. Interestingly enough, it was a widespread Edo Period view as well. Schoolchildren were called *terako*, literally "temple children," and schools were known as *terakoya*, though by then they had generally lost their earlier affiliation with temples.

They were private concerns, run in towns by professional teachers, in the countryside usually by retired village elders who taught at least the rudiments of reading, writing and Confucian morality, chiefly filial piety – to such effect that eighteenth-century Japan, for all its international isolation, was one of the most literate societies in the world. One rough estimate has it that, nationwide, forty percent of Edo Period boys and ten percent of girls – of all social classes – attended a terakoya for at least part of their childhood.

Here is the story of one who did not attend – not for lack of desire. Shika Noguchi was born in 1852 into a poverty-stricken farm family in rural northern Honshu in what is now Fukushima Prefecture. She took her first job at age six – watching over village children while their parents worked. When the grandmother who raised her fell ill and needed expensive medicine, twelve-year-old Shika went into service with a local landowner, whose wife kept her at fieldwork all day and at weaving straw baskets and sandals late into the night.

The local terakoya class was taught by a Buddhist priest named Unoura. Shika longed to go, but had no time. She approached the priest and begged him to write a *hiragana* primer for her. With this in hand, late at night, by moonlight, while the landowner's household slept, she would sit up in the kitchen tracing the characters over and over on a tray sprinkled with ash taken from the fireplace.

We know of Shika because of a subsequent development the little girl could not possibly have imagined – she grew up to become the mother of the world-famous bacteriologist Hideyo Noguchi (1876-1928), whose biographers have not failed to give the influence of his indomitable mother its due.

Two years after Noguchi's birth, ten years into the modernizing, Westernizing Meiji Period (1868-1912),

Japan played host to a British traveler named Isabella Bird. Among the new government's early reforms was compulsory primary education, enacted in 1872. In her 1885 book *Unbeaten Tracks in Japan*, Bird recorded her impressions of a village school she visited near Tokyo: "At 7 a.m. a drum beats to summon the children to school... Too much Europeanized I thought it, and the children looked very uncomfortable sitting on high benches in front of desks, instead of squatting native fashion... Obedience is the foundation of the Japanese social order, and with children accustomed to unquestioning obedience at home the teacher has no trouble in securing quietness, attention and docility. There was almost a painful earnestness in the old-fashioned faces which pored over the school-books; even such a rare event as the entrance of a foreigner failed to distract these childish students."

Would Bird be heartened or horrified to discover how far beyond "docility" Japanese children have evolved since then?

(2010)

Moon Over Matsushima

"God made me the messenger of the new heaven and the new earth of which He spoke in the Apocalypse."

– Christopher Columbus, 1498

"Here am I, in the Second Year of Genroku, suddenly taking it into my head to make a long journey to the far, northern provinces. I might as well be going to the ends of the earth!"

– Matsuo Basho, 1689

STRANGE, BY WESTERN STANDARDS, that pre-modern Japan's most famous traveler should have been a poet. The voyagers the West celebrates as explorers and discoverers were hard-headed seamen, rapacious adventurers, high-minded idealists – a mixed bag; but poetry?

Their inspiration lay elsewhere – in ambition stronger than prudence, in lusts deeper than fear. Fear of what? They hardly knew, which made it doubly fearful. It took Prince Henry the Navigator's fifteenth-century Portuguese sailors more than sixty years to inch their way down the unknown African coast – "for, said the mariners, this much is clear, that beyond [Morocco's

Cape Bojador] there is no race of men nor place of inhabitants… while the currents are so terrible that no ships having once passed the Cape will ever be able to return…" – so noted a contemporary chronicler.

Bartholomeu Dias, who rounded the continent's southern tip in 1488, was driven by courage of course, but also, lest his courage fail him, by a storm so terrible the crew "gave themselves up for dead." When the wind abated they found, to their astonishment, that the coast ran northeast. The Indian Ocean lay open before them, vast and uncharted. Somewhere out there were the fabulous "Indies," including "Cipangu," Japan – islands "most fertile," Marco Polo had reported two hundred years before, "in gold, pearls and precious stones, and they cover the temples and the royal residences with solid gold."

The cozy little world of medieval Christendom, three continents huddled around the Mediterranean with Paradise somewhere off to the east, was about to explode.

"On the 27th day of the third moon" of the second year of Genroku – May 16, 1689 – Basho (a pen name deriving from the *basho* banana plant near his cottage) set forth from Edo (Tokyo) on his most famous journey – a five-month trek north to Hiraizumi in present-day Iwate Prefecture, then southwest down the Sea of Japan coast to Ogaki near Lake Biwa. He was forty-five, a veteran of the road, with four poetic travel narratives already behind him. *Oku no Hosomichi (Narrow Road to the Deep North)* in 1694 became the fifth.

In the first, *Record of a Weather-Exposed Skeleton*, he describes his wanderlust: "Following the example of the ancient priest who is said to have traveled thousands of miles caring naught for his provisions and attaining the state of sheer ecstasy under the pure beams of the moon, I left my broken house on the River Sumida in [August 1684], among the wails of the autumn wind."

We gather from the title that he was not robust and his poem as he prepares to depart – "Determined to fall a weather-exposed skeleton…" – suggests awful, perhaps fatal rigors ahead. The anticipated harvest was poetry – not gold, spices, slaves, knowledge, trade routes, heathens converted to Christianity, or new lands won for his sovereign to reign over. Poetry: "Sheer ecstasy under the pure beams of the moon."

Basho surely never heard of Columbus and his new continent, or of Vasco da Gama who sailed round Africa and landed in India in 1498, or of Ferdinand Magellan who circumnavigated the globe in 1520-21. Basho's world, in physical terms, was far, far narrower than even the pre-Columbian Western world.

"China" was Basho's symbol for anything in it that was not Japan. He had never set eyes on China, never would, didn't want to. Had not Chinese and Japanese poets of old already captured its magnificence in verse? He left for the Deep North "dreaming of the moon over Matsushima"; nor did Matsushima disappoint him when he finally arrived: "Matsushima is indeed the most beautiful place in all Japan! It can easily hold its own with Lake Tung-ting and Lake Xi in China."

China meant more than dream-scenery to Columbus, and he had every intention of setting eyes on it. He envisioned a fabulous empire of gold, jewels, spices, inconceivable flora and fauna, possibly even the legendary Christian king known as Prester John, reportedly eager to unite with Western Christians against the infidel. China is where Columbus thought he was going when he sailed westward from Spain in August 1492; it's where he thought he was two months later when a Cuban "Indian" made a reference to a local region called "Cubanacan" and Columbus took him to mean "El Gran Can" – the Great Khan of Marco Polo's China. Thinking they were being escorted to the khan's palace, Columbus and his men arrived instead at a village of fifty palm-thatched huts, whose awed inhabitants received them as messengers from the sky. Basho would have been charmed.

Basho's "Cuba" – his "America" – was Japan's "far, northern provinces." That was as remote as a Japanese could legally venture in his day, and for nearly two centuries to come. The country had been sealed shut sixty years earlier by order of the Tokugawa shogunate. The policy was called *sakoku* – literally "closed country." Venturing overseas – or, having ventured, returning – was a capital offense.

Might not that cramp a wandering poet's style? Not Basho's. Far from straining at the bit, far from lusting for the great wide world from which his country's laws barred him, Basho paused at the Tokugawa shrine at Nikko on his way north to pay fulsome homage to "the most sacred of all shrines [whose] benevolent power prevails throughout the land embracing the entire people like the bright beams of the sun."

Politics aside, freedom is Basho's theme, embodied in his very trajectory. Heading north, writes Basho translator Nobuyuki Yuasa, meant "avoiding the familiar

Tokaido route." In the imagination of the people at least, the North was largely unexplored, and it represented for Basho all the mystery there was in the universe.

Symbolic gateway to this mystery was the Shirakawa Barrier, 180 km north of Edo, in present-day Fukushima Prefecture. An ancient defense against northern barbarians, it was a mere ruin in Basho's day, but as an *utamakura*, a place name with poetic associations, it was very much alive. "Had I a messenger I would send a missive to the capital!" wrote the poet Taira Kanemori at Shirakawa in the tenth century, by which time the barrier was already in disuse. The suggestion is of hopeless remoteness – but Basho, unlike Kanemori, was not ending his journey here. He was beginning it.

The West had its own version of sakoku. Scholars call it the "Great Interruption" – a thousand-year attempt, reinforced by all the supernatural terrors of the primitive Christian imagination, to squeeze the world into a shape consistent with Holy Writ. Jerusalem was "the navel of the world." "Six parts hast thou dried up," declared the apocryphal Book of Esdras – six parts of seven, that is: oceans hardly came into the picture at all. When they did, they led to the void or to Paradise.

Saint Brendan (484-578) sailed westward from Ireland to Paradise. So he said on his return, and he was believed. "His sacred island," writes historian Daniel Boorstin in *The Discoverers*, "remained plainly marked on maps for more than a thousand years, at least until 1759." Christopher Columbus, the "discoverer of America," made four voyages to his new continent without realizing that it was one. He thought it was Asia. But the puzzles and inconsistencies multiplied. His journals show him

51

suspecting the truth ("I believe this is a very great continent, until today unknown"), then veering away from it: "I am convinced it is the spot of the earthly paradise whither no one can go but by God's permission..." The great discoverer died in 1506, unenlightened by his discoveries.

By Basho's time, of course, most of the confusion had been sorted out. America was settled and thriving; the institutions and the thinking that were to spawn the American Revolution were well under way. Europe's fleets plied the oceans, its commerce spanned the globe. Even closed Cipangu had given the Dutch a foothold, at Nagasaki. The new world, vast beyond medieval imaginings, was slowly growing familiar.

Basho, meanwhile, plodded north. A famous contemporary portrait shows him in priestly garb, leaning on a stick, his feet shod in thin sandals, his disciple Sora following behind. He traveled mostly on foot, occasionally on horseback, a prematurely elderly man, feeble and frequently ill, braving the rigors of the road in pursuit of "the moon over Matsushima."

"Whatever such a mind sees is a flower," he had written earlier – "such a mind" meaning a mind in harmony with nature – "and whatever such a mind dream is the moon." In Basho, the stars pass almost unnoticed.

Did he know of the newly discovered shape and extent of the world? There is no indication he did, or that he cared about such things. Other matters preoccupied him, the smaller and quieter the better.

Born Matsuo Kinsaku in 1644 in the castle town of Ueno near Kyoto, he studied poetry as a child and, as a young man, cast off his samurai status to enter a temple. He moved to Edo, became a teacher of poetry, grew increasingly restless with social and poetic conventions, and drifted away from both, moving into a quasi-hermitage on the Sumida River and slowly, over the years, refining haiku from a facile social pastime into an art, mirroring "our everlasting self, which is poetry."

"What is the matter, you Christian men, that you so greatly esteeme so little portion of gold more than your own quietnesse..." So the sixteenth-century chronicler Peter Martyr records a young Indian reproaching a party of Spaniards quarreling over gold. A pity Basho never encountered these Indians. He would have liked them – and they him. "Since I had no interest whatever in keeping treasures, and since I was empty-handed, I had no fear of being robbed on the way."

As for "quietnesse," that was Basho's special discovery, and he gave it a significance beyond mere absence of noise:

Stillness –
the cicada's chirp
seeps into the rocks

He trudged miles, for months, through primitive country, in poor health – seeking no reward beyond "stillness." It must have been a marvelous stillness indeed, purchased at so high a cost.

Among the squabbling Spaniards was one Vasco Nunez de Balboa. The Indian, in Peter Martyr's report, continues, "I will shewe you a region flowing with golde, where you may satisfie your ravening appetites... When you are passing over these mountains… you will see another sea…"

Following the Indian's directions, Balboa and his party hacked their way across the Isthmus of Panama, passing "through inaccessible defiles inhabited by ferocious beasts… risking poisonous snakes and the arrows of unknown tribes." On September 25, 1513, they became the first Europeans to behold the Pacific Ocean. "Kneeling on the ground, [Balboa] raised his hands to heaven and saluted the… sea; according to his account he gave thanks to God and all the saints for having reserved this glory for him, an ordinary man…"

Basho immortalized lesser glory. From Yamagata, where he encountered the cicada, he trekked on to the Mogami River. "The river was swollen with rain, making the boat journey perilous." Of such scenes is haiku made.

Gathering the rains
of the wet season – swift
the Mogami River

(2003)

Confucius and the Soul of Japan

IS WHAT CONFUCIUS SAID TRUE? Can music, poetry and decorum govern the world? Do rulers, by cultivating benevolence in themselves, plant benevolence in their subjects, and harmony in their polity?

The chaos of our time hardly invites us to take such notions seriously. But Confucius' time was chaotic too. The ancient Chou dynasty was crumbling, upstarts vied for power, morality was breaking down.

In despair, a high government official proposed executing all wrongdoers. Confucius said, "In administering your government, what need is there to kill? Just desire the good yourself and the common people will be good."

The same official asked what to do about thieves. Confucius said, "If you yourself were not a man of desires" – corrupt, in other words – "no one would steal even if stealing carried a reward."

Asked why he did not take office, Confucius replied, "Simply by being a good son and friendly to his brothers a man can exert influence upon government."

A society, in Confucius' view, was an extended family in which, ideally, family relationships and family harmony prevailed. "A youth who does not respect his elders will achieve nothing when he grows up." A respectful son grows into a man worthy of respect and therefore a worthy ruler – of his family certainly, of society as a whole possibly. Rule meant, first and foremost, *self*-rule – self-cultivation.

Confucius. The name is so familiar that we are apt to forget how little we know the man, though thanks to cryptic snatches of his conversation recorded by his disciples in a book called the *Analects* (from a Greek word meaning "collection") he is, though elusive, not entirely unknowable.

As for his teachings, the general verdict throughout most of the revolutionary twentieth century was that they (or their derivatives, legitimate and bastard) had accomplished their civilizing mission millennia ago and were best relegated to the remote past, having long since grown moldy in the service of Asian autocrats – Japanese shoguns among them – who invoked him with relish, and continue to invoke him, for his supposed emphasis on unquestioning obedience.

The fragmentary nature of the *Analects* is conducive to the selective reading that autocrats have habitually given it. "Never disobey," said Confucius – it is one of his several definitions of filial piety, and sounds categorical enough. But he also said, in a passage less frequently honored with official quotation, "If a man is correct in his own person, then there will be obedience without orders being given; but if he is not correct in his own person, there will not be obedience even though orders are given."

"Correct" means, above all, "benevolent." Benevolence is easy: "Is benevolence really far away? No sooner do I desire it than it is here." But the desire for it, judging by its rarity, is difficult. It commits a ruler above all, but also human beings in general, to the quest for

56

moral perfection, to a "return to the observance of the rites through overcoming the self."

Few rulers in any era are up to such standards, and Confucius' impatience with those who are not is apparent in his advice to a disciple who asked how best to serve a prince: "Tell him the truth even if it offends him."

As for the rulers of his own day, "Oh," said Confucius, "they are of such limited capacity that they hardly count."

Almost alone among the ancient teachers of mankind, Confucius (K'ung Ch'iu in Chinese; Koshi in Japanese) was neither god nor prophet nor, in sharp contrast to his Taoist near-contemporary, Lao-tzu, mystic.

"Chi-lu asked how the spirits of the dead and the gods should be served," we read in the *Analects*. "The Master said, 'You are not able even to serve man. How can you serve the spirits?'"

"May I ask about death?"

"You do not even understand life. How can you understand death?"

Revere the gods and spirits, he taught, "but keep them at a distance." They are not man's immediate concern. Moral perfection, whose outward manifestation is "work[ing] for the things the common people have a right to," is its own reward. There is no hint in his teaching of any other reward, natural or supernatural.

The China into which Confucius was born in 551 BC was not really China. That name derives from the imperial Ch'in dynasty, whose harsh though brief militarist, legalist, bureaucratic rule three centuries later (221-207 BC) represented everything Confucius abhorred. Confucius was a relatively humble citizen of the "state" of Lu, an eastern backwater, one of the least among twelve semi-independent, strife-ridden dukedoms of the tottering Chou dynasty.

It was the Chou dynasty's golden age, five hundred years before his birth, that Confucius looked back to with longing and dreamed of reviving.

"I transmit but do not innovate," he said. What he sought to transmit were the rites, music and poetry that had prevailed in a time, semi-mythical, when rites, music and poetry had in effect ruled – primarily the poetry preserved in the *Book of Odes*, originating in the Golden Age and expressing the innocence to which Confucius aspired.

"When those above are given to the observance of the rites," Confucius taught, "the common people will be easy to command." Force is unnecessary. Law is superfluous. "There was nothing for him to do," said Confucius of the ruler of a state in which the Way of the ancient sage-kings prevailed, "but to hold himself in a respectful posture and to face due south," in accord with the traditions of ancient cosmology.

It was not the Way, however, but conditions approaching anarchy that prevailed in Confucius' own time. His father had been a soldier, a daring and conspicuous figure in the numerous wars of the period. Confucius was orphaned early.

"I was of humble station when young," he later told his disciples. "That is why I am skilled in many menial things. Should a gentleman be skilled in many things? No, not at all."

Very little is known of his early childhood, but "at fifteen," he said, "I set my heart on learning." What the impetus was we don't know, but his absorbing interest, the special focus of his studies, was *li* – "the rites." It is a problematic term. No English word quite does it justice, scholars say, and a tendency to translate it as "ritual" has helped fuel modern impatience with Confucius.

Some of the li-soaked sections of the *Analects* are undeniably tiresome, to our thinking.

"On going through the outer gates to his lord's court, [Confucius] drew himself in, as though the entrance was too small to admit him. When he stood, he did not occupy the center of the gateway; when he walked, he did not step on the threshold. When he went past [his lord's empty throne], his face took on a serious expression... When he lifted the hem of his robe to ascend the hall, he drew himself in, stopped inhaling as if he had no need to breathe..."

And so on – it's a long passage, and there are many others like it.

But, as David Hall and Roger Ames point out in an essay published in *Confucianism for the Modern World* (2003), "The *Analects* does not provide us with a catechism of prescribed formal conducts, but rather with the image of a particular historical person [i.e., Confucius] striving with imagination to exhibit the sensitivity to ritualized living that would ultimately make him the teacher of an entire civilization."

The outward manifestation matters less than the spirit animating it. "Appropriately performed," say Hall and Ames, "li elevates the commonplace and customary into something elegant and profoundly meaningful."

Once a disciple asked Confucius what he would do first if he were ever a ruler. "If something has to be put first," Confucius replied, "it is, perhaps, the rectification of the names."

The disciple thought Confucius was joking; it seemed rather a trivial thing – though it shouldn't to us, living as we do in an age of government by spokespersons and spin-doctors. Confucius (with some asperity at the disciple's "boorishness") explained: "When names are not correct, what is said will not sound reasonable; when what is said does not sound reasonable, affairs will not culminate in success; when affairs do not culminate in success, rites and music will not flourish; when rites and music do not flourish, punishments will not fit the crimes: when punishments do not fit the crimes, the common people will not know where to put hand and foot."

Note the absence of any mention, in connection with crime and punishment, of law.

Confucius was profoundly distrustful of laws. "If you use laws to direct the people," he said, "and punishments to control them, they will merely try to evade the laws, and will have no sense of shame. But if by virtue you guide them, and by rites you control them, there will be a sense of shame, and of right" – and social harmony will prevail.

Contemporaneous with Confucius were philosophers called Legalists. Their doctrine – the rule of law – seems, in light of future history, progressive, while Confucius' notion of "rites and music" strikes us as quaint, if not hopelessly reactionary.

But some modern psychologists are learning from the horrors of our time a new respect for Confucius.

Simon Leys, in an accompanying commentary to his translation of the *Analects*, quotes French psychologist Boris Cyrulnik: "When families are no longer able to generate rites that can interpret the surrounding world and transmit the parental culture, children find themselves cut off from reality, and they have to create their own culture – a culture of archaic violence...

"Incidences of incest are increasing," Cyrulnik continues, "because too many men no longer feel they are fathers. As family relationships have weakened and roles have changed, individuals do not see clearly what their proper place is. This is the symptom of a cultural breakdown."

"Can I not, perhaps," mused Confucius, "create another Chou in the east?" This was his life's mission, to recreate in the east – in his home state of Lu – his no doubt misty-eyed image of the golden age of the Chou dynasty founded by King Wen, King Wu and the Duke of Chou.

Intermittently, he assumed official positions under unsavory usurpers in order to further his goal. He gathered round him disciples – seventy-seven are known by name – who might in a sense be called co-conspirators. The conspiracy, in which trickery figured more than violence, was an attempt to undermine the usurpers and return power to the legitimate heirs of the House of Chou. It came undone, and Confucius fled. He spent most of his last years in exile in neighboring states, returning to Lu shortly before his death in 479 BC.

"For two thousand years," says Leys, "Confucius was canonized as China's First and Supreme Teacher. This is a cruel irony. Of course, Confucius devoted much attention to education, but he never considered teaching as his first and real calling. His first vocation was politics. He had a mystical faith in his political mission."

It failed. Never has the world known a Confucian state, if by that we mean what Confucius meant – a state governed by family relationships, nourished by benevolence and regulated by the poetry, music and rites of ancient sage-kings.

Korea under the Choson dynasty (1392-1910) is often said to have come closest, but what much of Asia got instead was Imperial Confucianism, a creation of China's Han dynasty (202 BC – 220 AD). The Ch'in dynasty, which the Han overthrew, had burned manuscripts associated with Confucius, but some survived to be favored by a leading Han court philosopher – who, circa 196 BC, provoked his emperor's impatience by vigorously advocating their official adoption.

"I conquered my empire on horseback," snapped the emperor, "and I will rule my empire on horseback." Replied the philosopher: "Your Majesty, one may conquer an empire on horseback but one may never rule an empire on horseback."

Very much struck by that, the emperor proceeded to offer the first official sacrifice – of an ox – to the tomb of Confucius. This may be said to mark the birth of official Confucianism, an unwieldy collage of Confucian principle, later reinterpretation and imperial expediency. It had an awesome future ahead of it, spreading its influence well beyond China's borders and becoming one of the most extensive and durable systems of government in world history – but it generally fell short when it came to benevolence.

"Confucius," says Leys bluntly, "was certainly not a Confucianist."

Indeed, the sage apparently died suspecting such would be the case. "I suppose I should give up hope," he sighed. "I have yet to meet the man who is as fond of virtue as he is of the beauty in women."

(2006)

How Japan and China
First Met

ADOPT "A CORRECT VIEW OF HISTORY," China and South Korea demand of Japan. Fair enough. We can all agree on the merits of a "correct view" of anything. The only difficulty is to define "correct."

As the intensifying acrimony unfolds over who did what to whom and how horribly, you'd almost think historical relations between the three countries began in 1895, when newly Westernized Japan defeated China in Korea, and ended in 1945 with Japan prostrate and guilty at the end of World War Two.

That was a fateful half-century, to be sure. But among ancient nations that have known each other a very, very long time, a "correct view" cannot be a short one.

To get the true flavor of things, we must go back to the beginning. It is hard to believe now, but some day – in seventeen centuries, perhaps? – Japan's wartime atrocities may seem as remote as, say Empress Jingu's fourth-century, semi-mythical invasion of the Korean kingdom of Silla, whose king, surrendering in abject terror (says the Japanese version), promised, "Not allowing the helms of our ships to become dry, every spring and every autumn we will send tribute of horse-combs and whips. And, without thinking the sea-distance a trouble, we will pay annual dues of male and female slaves..."

The Chinese had a name for the people of Japan long before the proto-Japanese had one for themselves. It was "Wa," or "Wo," written with a character that means "dwarf."

This hints at a perceived racial distinction, a perception supported by modern ethnology. The racial origins of the Japanese remain in dispute, but the complexity of the gene pool is generally acknowledged. Wherever their earliest ancestors may have come from, the Wa, their Chinese observers noted, "are divided into one hundred countries. Each year envoys from the Wa bring tribute."

So reads the first known description of Japan in history, written by a Chinese chronicler in AD 82, centuries before the Japanese were literate.

The "one hundred countries" may have been petty chiefdoms in northern Kyushu, or alternatively – scholarly controversy rages to this day – petty chiefdoms in "Yamato," the Japanese heartland in central Honshu. A century and a half later, a confederacy of some of these "countries" was ruled by the famous shaman-queen Himiko, or Pimiko, whose embassy to Chinese-occupied Korea in 238 appealed to the Wei Dynasty emperor for help against her hostile neighbor, the "country" of Kunu.

The Wei emperor Ming responded: "Herein we address Himiko, queen of Wa, whom we now officially call a friend of Wei... You live very far away across the sea; yet you have sent an embassy with tribute. Your loyalty and filial piety we appreciate exceedingly. We confer upon you, therefore, the title 'Queen of Wa, friendly to Wei.'"

The Chinese record of the transaction proceeds with an itemized list of gifts the emperor entrusted to Himiko's returning ambassadors: brocades, tapestries, gold and – most precious of all, perhaps – one hundred bronze mirrors. "You may exhibit them to your countrymen," the emperor concluded, "in order to demonstrate that our country thinks so much of you as to bestow such exquisite gifts upon you."

Chinese civilization was ancient long before Japan emerged from pre-civilized infancy. By 5000 BC the Chinese were organized in settled farming communities. By 1750 BC they had writing and bronze technology. By 700 BC they had iron – iron plows, iron weapons. Japan, all this time and for centuries to come, remained a Stone Age hunting-and-gathering backwater. Pottery is its most distinctive cultural artifact, its characteristic rope-pattern design giving the name Jomon (*jomon* means "rope-pattern") to the vast stretch of Japanese pre-history that does not draw to a close until the third century BC – when rice becomes the defining product.

Rice does not grow wild in the archipelago. It arrived, says one theory among many, via Korea from the Yangtze River basin in central China. Though rice was grown here and there by the late Jomon people, it was in the succeeding Yayoi Period (c.300 BC – AD 300) that wet rice cultivation became a way of life, making for the settled communities that are the basic prerequisite for civilization.

The Yayoi Period's creative surge was launched by a wave of Korean immigration that followed Chinese invasions under the imperial Han Dynasty (206 BC- AD 220). The newcomers brought not only advanced agricultural techniques but metal culture. Japan's prolonged Stone Age was over at last.

67

Bronze mirrors such as those conferred upon Himiko, decorated with mythological beasts (azure dragons, white tigers) and inscribed with Chinese poems, fill Yayoi Period burial sites in northern Kyushu. Graves are the temples and art museums of early societies. For centuries in China, mirrors had figured in Taoist rituals to ward off evil spirits. The shaman-chiefs of Wa used them for similar purposes – and for another as well: as symbols of recognition accorded by that inconceivably marvelous kingdom across the western sea. Chiefs who had them could overawe, overwhelm and overrule those who didn't.

Half a century after Himiko, the Wa were at least important enough to the Wei Dynasty (one of six to fill the vacuum left by the fall of the Han in AD 220) to figure in the late-third-century *History of Three Kingdoms*, written by a Wei historian named Chen Shou-yu.

Deriving his information primarily from a Wei embassy to the Wa "country" of Yamatai (Ye-ma-tai in Chinese, its location a subject of spirited academic controversy), Chen, in his chapter on "Eastern Barbarians," describes a settled, peaceful and productive society: "They are a long-lived race, and persons who have reached age 100 are very common. All men of high rank have four or five wives… The women are faithful and not jealous. There is no robbery or theft, and litigation is infrequent… Taxes are collected. There are markets in each province…"

The Wa, however, had "no oxen, horses… or sheep."

After the Wei mission to Yamatai, communication between the two countries lapsed. When it resumed nearly two centuries later, Japan had grown. Known then as Yamato (a native Japanese name whose similarity to Yamatai is apparently coincidental), it was ready to embark on a serious apprenticeship to Chinese civilization – a civilization that, transplanted eastward, was to attain its full Japanese flowering in eighth-century Nara.

Japan's early development was slowed by the same factor that drives its trade policies today: resource poverty.

With scarcely any iron and (until an eighth-century discovery) no copper at all, a metal culture was beyond its means before Chinese and Korean immigrants arrived to lead the way. The ensuing iron hunger brought Japan into close contact with Korea.

The Korean Peninsula then was divided chiefly among three kingdoms intermittently at war with one another: Kokuri in the north, Paikche in the southwest and Silla in the southeast. A fourth, Mimana, was a sliver of land between Paikche and Silla that may have been controlled by Yamato – if it existed. Scholars are not sure. Early Japanese history is a most uncertain field.

"The country produces iron," wrote Chen of southern Korea, "and the Wa all pursue and take it."

The official *Nihon Shoki*, a Chinese-style (and in fact Chinese-language) history compiled under imperial auspices in 720 AD, records this snatch of dialogue (dated 246 AD, but *Nihon Shoki* chronology is notoriously unreliable) between the king of Mimana and a Paekche envoy: "I have always heard," said the king, "that there is an honorable country in the east, but I have had no communication with it, and do not know the way. There is nothing but far seas and towering billows, so that in a large ship one can hardly communicate."

"Well then," replied the envoy, "for the present we cannot communicate."

There the matter ended for the time, but a few years later (in 252, according to the *Nihon Shoki*) the same Paekche envoy is described as regaling his Yamato hosts with tales of an "Iron Mountain" in Korea. This is the prologue to the supposed victorious invasion led, under "divine protection," by Empress Jingu – a legendary recasting, say modern scholars, of hazy events that occurred in the late fourth century.

Though evidently powerful, Yamato in its early phase was hardly civilized. We look back at fourth-century Japan and are astonished at how little progress it has made. A thousand years after Confucius and the Buddha and the founding of Rome there are still no cities to speak of, no roads or bridges worthy of the name, no writing. Even agriculture, ten thousand years old in the world at large, is here in its infancy.

Then came the fifth and sixth centuries, and our astonishment redoubles, for they are all that stand between barbarian Japan and the splendors of the Nara Period (710-794). How did it leap so far, so fast? The answer, in three words, is: China and Korea. More accurately: China *via* Korea.

From bronze mirrors and iron tools, the story now abruptly shifts to literature and religion. The year is 285 according to the *Nihon Shoki*, 405 by one of several modern reckonings. In any case it was during the reign of Empress Jingu's son Ojin.

"The king of Paekche," says the *Nihon Shoki*, "sent A-chik-ki with two quiet horses as tribute." A-chik-ki was a scholar, "able to read the [Chinese] classics."

In such casual terms is the advent of Japanese literacy recorded.

A-chik-ki was succeeded as court teacher by Wang-in, or Wani, of whom the *Nihon Shoki* says, "There was [no book] which he did not thoroughly understand." The guild of scribes he founded, staffed by immigrants, functioned as a court secretariat, keeping government records and drafting correspondence with the only foreign governments of whose existence early Japanese rulers seem aware: the Chinese and the Korean.

"Our land is remote, far across the sea," reads a memorial they wrote for Emperor Yuryaku in 478 to a Chinese court – one of several Chinese courts, for China was still in some disarray. "... Generation after generation our ancestors have paid homage to your court. Your subject, ignorant though he may be, has succeeded to the throne and is fervently devoted to Your Sovereign Majesty. Everything he has is at Your Majesty's disposal..."

The obsequious tone is in stark contrast to what was soon to come. Momentous developments lay ahead. China, re-unified in 589 under the Sui Dynasty, regained and then surpassed its ancient Han Era splendor. And Japan's Asuka Enlightenment, occurring almost simultaneously, inspired the breathtaking confidence which emboldened the Prince Regent Shotoku, the leading spirit of the age, to address the Sui emperor as an equal – "Child of Heaven" to "Child of Heaven."

The Asuka Enlightenment can be summed up in one word: Buddhism. Its introduction to Japan originates in an embassy from Paekche arriving in 552 (538, say some) to request military assistance for its endless wars with Silla. The ambassadors, says the *Nihon Shoki*, presented the Emperor Kinmei with "an image of [the Buddha] in gold and copper, several flags and umbrellas, and a number of volumes of sutras."

"This doctrine is amongst all doctrines the most excellent," reads the accompanying memorial. "But it is

71

hard to explain, and hard to comprehend." Comprehended or not, though, "every prayer is fulfilled."

The emperor "leaped for joy": still, he hesitated to embrace the "wonderful doctrine." Court factions supported it against other factions that staunchly defended the native gods. A brief war settled the issue in 587. The Soga clan, of Korean origin, was victorious, and the Buddhism it patronized was officially adopted. The Asuka-dera Temple built in 596 in Asuka village in present-day Nara Prefecture was Japan's first large-scale Chinese-style building. Forty-five others followed, built by Korean craftsmen and staffed by Korean priests, before the Asuka Period ended in 645.

Prince Shotoku is best remembered today for his "Constitution" of seventeen injunctions, traditionally dated 604. However bland they may sound to us ("Harmony is to be cherished… When an imperial command is given, obey with reverence... Punish that which is evil and encourage that which is good…"), their Buddhist and Confucian notions of morality and government represent innovations which George Sansom, the eminent British diplomat-historian, goes so far as to call "revolutionary."

They owe "nothing to indigenous thought," Sansom writes (in *Japan: A Short Cultural History*). "Hidden in these apparently harmless exhortations to governors and governed is a new view of the state, for while they exact obedience from inferiors to superiors, they insist equally upon the duties of superiors to inferiors, and, what is most significant of all, they enunciate very clearly the theory of a centralized state."

The theory was within a generation to be practice – or at least the basis for practice. A central, bureaucratic,

Chinese-style state, Confucian in its identification of the emperor with the Mandate of Heaven (though not in its shielding of the emperor from the consequence of misrule – namely forfeiture of the Mandate of Heaven) is in fact what emerged from a movement that began in 645 under the name *Taika*, Great Reform.

The palace coup that launched it was a nasty affair, neither Buddhist nor Confucian in its gruesomeness, and one can only wonder what the gentle Shotoku (who died in 622) would have thought of the Soga potentate being hacked to death in the presence of the empress in the name of ideas which he, Shotoku, had propagated.

Be that as it may, the Great Reform marks the beginning of Japan as a state – as opposed to a loose assemblage of clans.

Prominent among the officials who founded it and made it work (most imperfectly, for Japanese conditions were worlds apart from the Chinese setting in which it had evolved) were men who had spent decades in China as students in the two missions dispatched by Shotoku in 607 and 608.

One may well imagine the astonishment of the Sui emperor Yang-ti when, in 607, Shotoku's envoy, Ono no Imoko, presented a memorial containing the words, "The Child of Heaven in the land where the sun rises addresses the Child of Heaven in the land where the sun sets."

Was Wa being deliberately insulting, or did it simply not know its place?

"If memorials from barbarian states are written by persons who lack propriety," Yang-ti instructed his officials, "do not accept them."

Somehow the clash was smoothed over. And it was Yang-ti, not Shotoku, who was to get his comeuppance, for Yang-ti's disastrous military campaigns against Koguryo in Korea brought the Sui Dynasty to an abrupt end in 618. It was followed by the even more magnificent Tang. No nation has ever set out with more eager, if patronizing, generosity than Tang China to teach the arts of civilization to its less-favored neighbors.

And no acolyte nation was ever so avid a pupil as the newly sinicized Japan of the eighth and early ninth centuries. It is a development well worth pondering in our quest for that elusive "correct view" of history.

Chang'an, capital of Tang China, was in the seventh and eighth centuries the largest city in the world. Nara, with its rectangular layout and broad avenues, was modeled on it but hardly measured up. Immense by Japanese standards, and three times the size of nearby Fujiwara, the capital it replaced, Nara would all the same have struck a Chinese visitor from the metropolis as paltry. It had 200,000 people; Chang'an had 1.2 million. Nara, unlike Chang'an, had no high walls, no brick and stone buildings, no soaring tile roofs; above all, perhaps, it hosted no steady stream of ambassadors, traders, monks and students from all over the known world, as Chang'an did – awestruck Japanese among them.

What Nara did have, beginning with is founding in 710, was a profusion of court officials steeped in Confucian protocol. They wore Chinese robes, wrote Chinese-language memorials, drafted Chinese-style laws and bore the Chinese ranks imported a century earlier by Prince Shotoku – "virtue," "benevolence," "propriety," "sincerity" and so on, each rank subdivided into "greater" and "lesser." Some six thousand of these officials governed a Japanese population of roughly five million.

Japan's sinicization had begun in earnest with the bloody palace coup that in 645 launched the Great Reform. The rising power of China under the Tang Dynasty was terrifying. In 660 it swallowed the Korean kingdom of Paekche. Would Japan be next?

"Everyone here is saying that Japan will soon be faced with Heaven's retribution," a Japanese official of the time recorded in his diary.

Sinicization was inspired by much the same feeling that drove nineteenth-century Westernization: the enemy could only be resisted with its own techniques and its own weapons. As it happened, the dreaded Tang invasion never came. The relationship that developed between the two countries was not belligerent-to-belligerent, or overlord-to-vassal, but the most extraordinary one, quite unprecedented in the history of international relations, of teacher-to-pupil. Japan, it might be said, attended the Chinese school of civilization in Chang'an.

Between 607 and 838, Japan sent nineteen missions to China – on average, one every twelve years. Knowledge was the principal goal. Priests studied Buddhism; officials, government; doctors, medicine; painters, painting; and so on. To gauge the eagerness with which the wisdom China symbolized was pursued, we need only consider the hazards of the sea crossing. Nearly a third of those who set out never returned.

China-bound fleets were called "the Four Boats." Four boats departed together; it was a rare and lucky voyage that brought all four safely to their destination at the mouth of the Yangtze River. The East China Sea is stormy, and Japanese shipbuilding and navigation were hopelessly inadequate for the 800-km crossing. It is surprising that Japan, a maritime nation after all, was so far behind contemporary Chinese, Koreans, Arabs and Vikings in this regard. The sea is one challenge the early Japanese never rose to.

And so in flat-bottomed boats caulked with seaweed — "a mere assembly of planks and poles," as twentieth-century historical novelist Ryotaro Shiba put it — with primitive sails that stood little chance against the brisk breezes and storm winds of the open sea, trusting navigation that owed nothing to astronomy and much to Chinese yin-yang divination, the acolytes and envoys and crew (including large numbers of oarsmen for when the sails gave out) set forth, about a hundred men in each boat, grimly resigned to the fact that their chances of surviving were not high.

Shiba gives us a graphic description of one such voyage in his book *Kukai the Universal*, a biography of the priest Kukai (774-835).

Kukai, better known as Kobo Daishi, traveled to Chang'an in 804 to study the esoteric Buddhist doctrine known in Japanese as Shingon (True Word). Its outstanding features are dramatic ritual and an optimistic belief that men and women in this life, in this world, in the flesh, are capable of attaining Buddhahood.

The fleet with which Kukai sailed left the port of Naniwazu, near present-day Osaka, on May 14. (Had Japanese sea captains mastered the winds they would have known that spring was no time to sail; the autumn winds are more favorable.) On Kukai's boat was the government envoy, Fujiwara no Kadonomaro, who, in keeping with the custom among envoys, changed his name to the more Chinese-sounding Kano. There was a stop at Kyushu to pick up additional passengers, among them the monk Saicho, with Kukai one of the most innovative and influential clerics of the time.

76

Then the Four Boats headed west into the East China Sea. At the sight of the Goto Islands, the westernmost extremity of Japanese territory, some passengers were driven mad with longing, writes Shiba, citing contemporary annals.

In good weather, a crossing would take ten days. Kukai's boat took thirty-four. There was a storm. The four boats soon lost sight of each other. Conditions on board were miserable – short rations, dysentery, depression. The priests chanted sutras day and night. The tempest blew them of course. They landed at last in Fuzhou in today's Fujian Province, a good 500 km south of the Yangtze.

It was semi-barbarous country; no one was on hand to receive them. They made their exhausted way to the provincial capital, only to be taken for smugglers. Kano came forward.

"I am the envoy representing the Japanese government," Shiba has him declare. But his Chinese failed to pass muster; typically, he owed his post not to his ability but to birth and connections. Compelled to state his case in writing, he presented document after document – in language so coarse, alas, that he might well have been a smuggler.

Fortunately, Kukai, a graduate of the Nara university and one of Japan's best sinologists, was at hand. He knew how to indite a Chinese diplomatic missive.

"Lofty mountains, though mute," he wrote, "are so attractive to beasts and birds that they endeavor to reach them even from afar with indefatigable eagerness... Likewise, even savages beyond the borders, enticed by the virtuous illumination upheld by the Chinese Emperor, are intent on reaching his land in defiance of all the dangers they must encounter on their way."

This was what the Chinese wanted to hear. The strangers were admitted without further ado. Ahead of them lay an arduous 2700-km trek – by boat, on foot, on horseback, in carts, through mountains, along canals whose engineering was a marvel but whose filth left the fastidious Japanese aghast – to Chang'an. Arriving at last, the travelers were overjoyed to hear that another of the four boats had preceded them. Of the remaining two there was no word. Later it would be learned that one of them had run aground, without loss of life, on a South Sea island. The other was never heard of again.

Most acolytes remained in China twenty years. Kukai stayed two. Far more advanced to begin with than the average student, and a far quicker learner, he not only mastered with astonishing speed the subtleties of the doctrine he had made up his mind to introduce to his countrymen, but he seems also to have found ample time for sightseeing.

His curiosity was boundless, and Chang'an – "a world exposition of thought," Shiba calls it – could not fail to stoke it. Studying, preaching, writing and praying in Chang'an were Muslims, Nestorian Christians, Zoroastrians and Manicheans from all over western and central Asia. Kukai wandered the city, seeking out the new and the strange. From Indian monks he learned Sanskrit, the first Japanese to master the language. Truly, one breathed a more expansive air here than in Japan.

Chang'an offered, and Kukai was eagerly open to, experiences of all kinds, not only religious. "One of the places he enjoyed visiting," writes Shiba, "was the West Market... It was interesting to see how a caravan that had been traveling all the way from lands unknown to him removed the bundles from the camels' backs. Another attraction was an open-air show of Persian girls dancing."

All this must have astonished Kukai – not because he was a monk but because he was from remote, insular Japan.

He returned home in 806 to found a Shingon temple complex on Mount Koya, in today's Wakayama Prefecture. In 838, the missions to China abruptly ceased. The Tang empire was crumbling, piracy was rising, and in any case the time had come for Japan to withdraw and assimilate the vast amount it had learned.

Withdrawal and assimilation are the themes of the Heian Period, a four-hundred-year surge of cultural creativity that began with the relocation of the capital to Kyoto in 794. Assimilating, Japan diverged. Heian was in a sense Japan's cultural declaration of independence from China, the first instance of an oft-remarked national genius for borrowing foreign forms and making something totally unique of them. The eleventh-century *Tale of Genji*, literary climax of the age, has no Chinese prototype. Many call it the world's first novel.

Official relations with China would not resume for five hundred years.

(2006)

Pop Went the Culture, 400 Years Ago

POP CULTURE. Japan's today is thriving, vibrant, spreading, turning people the world over into manga/anime freaks, costume players.

It's a new role for this once introverted, quietly workaholic nation. As recently as the 1980s, "culture" in Japan meant, if not corporate culture, high culture. Pop culture – culturally if not commercially – was peripheral. Now it is central, one of the few buoyant sectors in a society that otherwise seems to have lost its way.

Four hundred years ago there lived a woman who might have foreseen it. She launched it. Popular culture before her is an oxymoron. Japanese culture was ancient, elegant, stately, nuanced, refined, classical, exclusive. The rude masses had no part in it. They had their entertainments, circus-like and bawdy, courtesy of wandering musicians, dancers, ballad chanters, puppeteers, acrobats, swordsmen, animal trainers and the like, but if culture implies something transcending mere boisterousness, little of this qualified.

Japan's popular culture was born in a makeshift semi-outdoor theater on the banks of the Kamo River in Kyoto in 1604 – not far from the local execution grounds. Experts might balk at so sharp a turning point, but with due allowances made for gradual evolution and unsung forerunners, a dance spectacle staged there and then seems to mark a break with the past and a stride into the future. Modern anime fans would have found it right up their alley.

The mastermind was a dancer named Izumo no Okuni (c.1571-c.1615). She had grown up a shrine maiden doing devotional dances, and graduated to the river and other venues where she and the troupe she trained and led entertained the masses with songs, skits, flamboyant costumes and sexual innuendo – cross-dressing, for instance. She danced at court too, but her popular performances were described as *kabuki* – meaning "weird."

A collaborator who may or may not have been her lover was a dashing warrior named Nagoya Sanzaburo, known for wit, grace and a penchant for outlandish Portuguese attire – Portuguese traders and missionaries were then making early inroads. Sanzaburo was stabbed to death in a quarrel with another samurai. "A few months later," writes Mark Weston in *Giants of Japan* (1999), "in the middle of a performance, a handsome young man wearing fashionable Portuguese garb leapt onto Okuni's stage and demanded to see her, claiming to be Sanzaburo's ghost. The audience quickly realized that the actor playing the ghost was none other than Okuni herself, and erupted in cheers. For several minutes 'Sanzaburo' danced sensuously with the actress playing Okuni, until finally an angry hunchback drove 'Sanzaburo' back to the underworld."

Heard the one about the woman who cut off her nose? It's from Japan's first bestseller, a humor anthology published anonymously in 1615 under the title *Today's Tales of Yesterday.*

The woman's husband was ill, dying. The thought that she might remarry was darkening his last hours. Remarry? Never, she vowed. She would shave her head, become a nun, pray for the repose of his soul. The husband was moved, but not satisfied. Shaved hair grows back; a woman's heart is weak. It was a lot to ask, he admitted, but would she cut off her nose? That would reassure him, and he could die at ease.

Very well, said the wife.

To everyone's surprise, the husband recovered – a happy turn of fortune's wheel, except that he was now the husband of a noseless woman. "I am ashamed to tell you this," he said, "but seeing your face makes me wish I were dead. There is no kind way to say it: I want you to leave."

She protested; he insisted. The case ended up in court. He told his story, she told hers. The magistrates deliberated and reached their decision: "Off with his nose!" And so it was done. "Hand in hand, the noseless man and the noseless woman returned home and lived happily ever after without incident."

Once upon a time – this is from *Tales of the Floating World* (1666) by one of the first authors from the Edo Period (1603-1867) whose name survives, a onetime Buddhist priest named Asai Ryoi – a certain Hyotaro, scion of a Kyoto merchant house, became a slave to pleasure, specifically the varieties on offer at Shimabara, Kyoto's licensed erotic quarter.

One courtesan in particular consumed his attention, his energy, his fortune: "Being promised her true love until the end of time, he became so intoxicated with joy as to think less of his own life than of dirt. And all the

83

while he was being fawned on and flattered by the hired jesters.."

His family remonstrated with him: "By her nature, a courtesan is a woman who… adorns herself, and so is quite alluring… her lips languorous like a loose-wound spool, the fragrance of her perfume reaching to the skies. And how lovely when she moves, swaying back and forth; truly she could easily be mistaken for the living incarnation of the Amida Buddha! Compared with this creature, a man's wife can hardly seem to be more than a salted fish long past its prime!"

Well! – that'll kick the nonsense out of the young fool.

"And the thankfulness you feel," the family elder continued, "just to hear the sound of her voice! What great priest could bestow on you words of enlightenment equal to this?… So please," he concluded, "we beseech you, cease this folly!"

A moral sermon in which the irresistibility of pleasure is emphasized to sound a warning risks going badly astray.

"Truly," replied Hyotaro, "I am most grateful for your kind advice."

Whereupon he "hurried out on his way to the Shimabara and, before long, using up all he had, ended up as yet another of those thread-bare bums, to the tune of the samisen's '*te-tsuru-ten*'!"

Edo Japan made a startling discovery starkly at odds with the grimly authoritarian current of the times – fun.

Fun sounds like something spontaneous; in Japan it had to be discovered, or invented. Prior to the Edo Period, this warrior-based, war-racked, fastidiously ceremonial society "had lived as though in a graveyard," as the eminent American orientalist Wm. Theodore de Bary puts it.

Five developments permitted the rising of the dead that in turn generated Japan's first ever pop culture – peace, a prosperous and expanding merchant class, mass literacy, money and printing.

All appeared suddenly, transforming stately old Japan out of recognition – just as, four hundred years later, the Japan of militarism and *yamatodamashii* (Japanese spirit) was transformed by a postwar infusion of American mass culture.

The peace was imposed by a regime whose prime concern was to stifle any threat – real, potential or imaginary – to its own supremacy. The ruling Tokugawa shoguns carried conservatism to the extreme of closing the country to the outside world for more than two hundred years.

In the resulting hothouse atmosphere, literacy was a veritable explosion. Print was the new medium of the day, the cyberspace of late pre-modernity; it spoke to, for and of the masses, conferring upon them something they'd never had – status, significance.

Prior to the seventeenth century, most people, samurai included, were illiterate. Warriors at war perhaps don't need letters; warriors edgily at peace do, if they are not to be ungovernable. Shoguns and feudal lords were accordingly energetic builders of schools. With astonishing rapidity, literacy took hold and filtered down the social strata. By the mid 1650s almost everyone except the very poor and, for a time, most women, was literate and hungry for books.

A new technology – woodblock printing, better suited than movable type to Japanese writing – churned them out. Urban Tokugawa Japan was awash in cheap, illustrated paperbacks, forerunners of today's manga.

This was a blow to the itinerant lute-playing blind minstrels, traditional entertainers of an earlier day with their epic war ballads (the thirteenth-century *Tales of the Heike* was a perennial favorite). But all change impoverishes some while enriching others. Writing and publishing became profitable ventures.

As for money, Japan's economy had long been rice-based. The first native gold and silver coins (Chinese coins had circulated much earlier) were minted at the end of the sixteenth century, and favored the budding though officially despised merchant class. But the significant date for our purpose is 1636, when the shogun began minting bronze coins called *zeni*. This was pocket money, small change.

Pop culture is impossible without it.

Armed insurrection was one perennial Tokugawa fear. Sex was another. The erotic impulse is unruly, anarchic. You never know what people under its spell might do. Early kabuki unsettled the shoguns and aroused their containing instinct. Okuni's dance troupe was all female; likewise its imitators and successors. They were wildly popular. Fights broke out as men competed for their favors. The spectacles were banned. Boys' kabuki arose to fill the void. Same problem, same solution.

The rumblings of discontent that followed were so ominous that the shogun relented – somewhat. Kabuki was to be strictly adult, strictly indoor and, onstage, strictly male (the leading *onnagata*, male actors who played women, did more to set female fashions than any woman), with a (theoretically) de-eroticized story line to be given prominence over pure dance.

Similar treatment was accorded the numerous and scattered brothels – they were licensed and concentrated in one area of each town or city. The result, by the mid-seventeenth century, was the development of two urban *akusho* (bad places) – the theater distinct and the pleasure quarter. They were the two main venues of Edo Period pop culture. There wasn't much fun outside of the akusho but plenty of it in them.

In the quarters men loved and were loved, or at least indulged, and in the kabuki and puppet theaters they saw themselves and their passions writ large, frivolity heightened to drama, lovers to heroes, love to tragedy.

True, the courtesans' favors were bought and sold; true also that the courtesans, however cultured and artistically gifted, were what a later age would call sex slaves. But marriage in pre-modern Japan was a perfunctory, unsatisfying affair, designed for the begetting of family heirs. Love, or at least the possibility of it, was a breathtaking discovery. Look what it did to poor Hyotaro.

Licensed quarters sprang up across the country. Even a modest town was likely to have one. The three largest were Yoshiwara in Edo, Shinmachi in Osaka and Shimabara in Kyoto. Here men posed, swaggered, strutted, made extravagant fools of themselves. Edo pop literature spoofed the rutting male with gusto. The goal was to acquire *tsu* – sophistication. The role model was the urbane playboy who knew the quarters and their intricate customs, knew how to talk to courtesans and get his way with them.

Sharebon (books of wit and fashion), wildly popular from the mid-eighteenth century, wickedly satirized the "half-tsu" – the self-deluded buffoon whose pretensions to sophistication were ludicrous but also educational, exposing to readers the blunders to be avoided en route to full tsu-hood.

A literary romp through the Yoshiwara, titled *The Playboy Dialect* (1770), author unknown, is considered the first true sharebon. A half-tsu character called Man-About-Town, a somewhat down-at-heel samurai, shepherds a rich merchant's innocent young son to the quarter, his eagerness to impress pathetically endearing. They enter the quarter, Man-About-Town pattering non-stop: "If anybody catches sight of me, they'll all flock around and kick up a fuss! Tonight I'd like us to amuse ourselves quietly, just the two of us. My, the place looks deserted tonight! What teahouses shall we go to? I know so many places..."

His unawareness that teahouse proprietresses and courtesans of various ranks are laughing at him behind his back is touching; his mortification at being unrecognized in premises where he has claimed a vast reputation reminds us of the timeless nature of human foibles, however exotic the environment.

In style and content, Edo pop culture is everything ancient Japanese culture was not, and much of what today's pop culture is – raw, garish, bursting with life and disdainful of nuance.

Grilled and Basted Edo-Born Playboy – there's a title to reckon with! It's a *kibyoshi* ("yellow booklet," so called from the characteristic color of the cover) that appeared in three slim volumes in1785. Kibyoshi were similar to sharebon but more copiously illustrated (more manga-like), more sharply satiric, less didactic.

The basted playboy is the creation of an acknowledged master of the genre, Santo Kyoden

(1761-1816). The hero, or anti-hero, has the right name – Enjiro, meaning sexy. And he has the right background – only son of a rich and indulgent merchant father, owner of the Wanton Shop, purveyor of Western luxuries obtained via the Dutch United East India Company, one of very few foreign concerns permitted to trade, under tight restrictions, in the otherwise closed country.

Enjiro should have it made, but it's no use – the girls don't like him. Still, why should that matter? What a determined man can't get one way, he can get another – can't he? When personal charms fail, money succeeds – doesn't it? Especially if, as with Enjiro, the quest is more for a lover's reputation than for a lover's love.

He has two rather disreputable friends – a playboy named Kinosuke and a jester, Shian. Under their wise and seasoned guidance, he sets to work. Every great lover, they advise him, has names of women tattooed all over him. That's the first thing he sees to, gamely enduring the pain in pursuit of his ideal. Via Shian, he pays a geisha fifty gold coins to pretend she's in love with him. For fifty gold coins she'll do anything. She sobs, debases herself, threatens suicide. When no one notices, Enjiro pays to have the affair written up in a broadsheet. To no avail. Edo is busy; Edo has no time for Enjiro.

He showers money on a top-ranking Yoshiwara courtesan, hires a "wife" to pretend she's jealous, pays some street toughs to beat him up (because in kabuki all irresistible lovers get beaten up), persuades his father to disown him (because in kabuki all profligate sons get disowned); the soft-hearted father at last reluctantly agrees to a seventy-five-day disownment), pays geisha to feign distress at his poverty, stages a love-suicide with the Yoshiwara courtesan (with Kinosuke and Shian standing by to intervene at the last moment) – and so on.

Somehow, nothing takes. Enjiro is one of those people nobody cares about, and nothing he does makes any difference. He and the courtesans are proceeding with their mock suicide when two masked robbers set upon them and drag them off – home, it turns out; the robbers are none other than Enjiro's father and an employee.

Sobered, Enjiro sees the folly of his ways. He and the courtesan marry. In due course he inherits the business and – who would have imagined? – settles down and matures into a shrewd, thrifty, classic Edo Period merchant!

The first Edo writer to treat love outside the pleasure quarters (not that he failed to treat it inside them as well) was the literary phenomenon Ihara Saikaku (1642-93). He was Japan's first writer with a nationwide readership. His popularity was enormous, his output no less so, though only long after his own time did anyone see greatness in him, and his writing – funny and tragic and hopeful and despairing all at once, sometimes in a single sentence – did much to shape the notoriously flamboyant Genroku Era (1688-1703).

Saikaku wrote of everything he knew, and he seemed to know everything. Born in Osaka of merchant stock, he flung himself and his myriad characters – male and female, heterosexual and homosexual, merchant, samurai, priest, yokel, courtesan, virgin, housewife – into the "endless stream of love on which [people] might embark with all their cares and float as light as bubbles through the Floating World."

Rules governing conduct in the pleasure quarters were strict in their own way, but the worst a man risked in breaking them – it was bad enough, of course – was ridicule. The shogunate had so far compromised with human passion as to give it these enclosed spaces to play in. Outside the quarters – no compromise and no play.

Love was dangerous. It was criminal. "Item one. Illicit intercourse," reads a Tokugawa statute. "Persons such as those who have engaged in illicit intercourse with their master's daughter, or who have attempted such: Death... Persons such as those who commit adultery with their master's wife, or with their teacher's wife: Death for both the man and the woman."

Saikaku's heroes and heroines – "bodies... stretched upon the rack of love" – love feverishly, compulsively, desperately, courting death knowingly and not caring because it's inevitable, it's worth it, and when the time comes they die bravely and proudly, teenage plebeian girls no less than adult plebeian men doing honor to the time-honored samurai tradition of "holding life lighter than a feather."

Thus we have Osan, one of Saikaku's *Five Women Who Love Love* (1686). We glimpse her first as a thirteen-year-old seen through the eyes of a group of young Kyoto rakes lounging about, eyeing the passing women. "Thanks to large inheritances, they could spend every day in the year seeking their own pleasure... Night or day, girls or boys, it made no difference."

Osan wins the lads' impromptu beauty contest hands down, but shortly afterwards marries the local almanac-maker and settles down. She's a steady and faithful wife – but passion will have its way. She loses her head and elopes with a shop clerk, a rather unappealing figure, seen from outside – but, explains Saikaku, "There is no logic in love."

Death rears its head from the start. Says Osan to herself, like one swept away by the tide, "I may as well abandon myself to this affair, risk my life, ruin my reputation, and take Moemon as my companion on a journey to death."

Is this despair, or joy? To make a long and wonderful story shorter than it deserves to be, the couple is discovered in their rural hiding place and hauled back, their sentence a foregone conclusion: "There was no room for mercy in view of their crime. When the judicial inquiry was duly concluded, the lovers... were paraded as an example before the crowds along the way to Awadaguchi [the execution ground], where they died like dewdrops falling from a blade of grass."

The Saikaku of the puppet theater, as we might call him, was Chikamatsu Monzaemon (1635-1725). Unlike Saikaku, Chikamatsu was samurai-born, but he too invested his plebeian heroes and heroines with the ultimate samurai virtue — an indifference to death that sometime seems almost a courtship of it, though in the service of love rather than of a feudal lord.

Love suicide is a recurring theme. What else can a man and a woman do in a world so inhospitable to the deepest human feelings?

"Did our promises of love hold only for this world?" exclaims the courtesan Ohatsu to the merchant Tokubei. Of course not. Tokubei is too poor to buy her contract and prevent a richer, craftier merchant from having her. And so, "Farewell to this world, and to the night farewell!... How sad is this dream of a dream!" Tokubei plunges a dagger into the throat of the woman he loves, and — "Must I lag behind you? Let's draw our last breaths together" — immediately cuts his own throat.

First staged in 1703, *The Love Suicides at Sonezaki* was based on an actual incident and inspired others. Love suicide became an epidemic, one following another. Fashions change, but the lure of fashion is constant, common to pop culture then and now.

How did this incendiary mass entertainment survive the censorship of a censorious, rigidly Confucian regime?

At times, it didn't.

As the merchant class rose the samurai fell, becoming themselves addicted to the character-corroding, fortune-depleting pleasures proliferating around them. The shogunate responded with what historian George Sansom called "an inky cloud of sumptuary edicts against extravagances of every kind."

An analogy is the determination of repressive societies today to censor the Internet. It's hit and miss. Sometimes it works, sometimes it doesn't.

In 1722, erotic literature was banned; in 1723, so was the dramatization of love suicides. The bans were effective for a while, until eventually writers and producers found ways around them; the bans were reinforced and the cycle began all over again. Some writers and publishers were arrested, some books suppressed, but in the long run, what are moral injunctions against the passions of an Osan, an Ohatsu, a Tokubei?

Edo pop culture, prototype of our own, is in one sense its opposite. Ours is an escape from dull mundanity into fantasy. Edo's was a discovery of – at times a desperate plunge into – the once-disdained pleasures of this world.

The scholar de Bary, writing of Saikaku's treatment of "the search for happiness in love," observes, "What at first sight seems no more than the universal preoccupation of man is soon seen to have a special quality, an extraordinary intensity akin to religious feeling."

Love was more than pleasure – it was salvation. The overarching metaphor is the *ukiyo*, the "floating world" and its twin meanings – floating in the Buddhist sense of ephemeral, and in the pop-culture sense of euphoric.

We come now to the *Floating World Bathhouse* – and would that space permitted us more time here! Edo in the early nineteenth century had more than six hundred public bathhouses. *Floating World Bathhouse* (1809) is a kibyoshi by Edo native, Edo writer, Edo bookseller Shikitei Sanba (1776-1822).

"Public baths," he wrote, "are the shortest route there is to moral and spiritual enlightenment... Both master and servant stand naked after they've washed away the grime of greed and worldly desires and rinsed themselves with fresh water – and you can't tell whom is which!

"Naked, the lustiest young bathers feel bashful and hold towels over their private parts. Fierce warriors, washing themselves off before bathing, endure the hot water splashed by others onto their heads and resign themselves to the ways of crowded places. Even irritable toughs with spirits and gods tattooed on their arms say 'Pardon please'... Where else but in a public bath can such virtues be found?"

Nowhere else, more's the pity. "The sign at the bathhouse entrance tells bathers, 'Full payment each time,' and helps them realize that life is short and comes only once."

The spirit of Edo pop – and of our pop too – in a nutshell.

(2011)

94

Holy Fools

RYOKAN THE POET wasn't much of a thinker – or so he thought, for he called himself Taigu, Great Fool, apparently in all sincerity. He didn't think; he lived. He summed up his life in a poem, which begins, "Rags and tatters, rags and tatters, rags and tatters." Was he complaining? Of his poverty, perhaps, or his loneliness? On the contrary. He was celebrating them.

Poverty was his wealth, solitude his company. He was a strange man, and though he lived on the threshold of modern times (1758-1831), the modern spirit is alien to him, and he to it. Modern times seem so full it is hard to believe that anything at all is excluded from them. Only Emptiness is. Rags and tatters have no place among us – no happy place, at least.

And laughter. We moderns laugh only at humor. That is not how the sages of old laughed. Ryokan's poetic precursor and teacher was a Chinese hermit of the Tang Dynasty (618-907) named Han-shan. Little is known about him. He is generally associated with his fellow recluse, Shih-te. Artists love drawing them, usually together. Among the numerous surviving portraits is a diptych by the twelfth-century painter Yen Hui. The monks' robes hang loose about them. Their hair is matted and unkempt. Han-shan leans on a broom. And they are laughing – laughing uproariously, laughing hideously.

"There is something in their transcendental air of freedom," observes Zen master Daisetz T. Suzuki, "which attracts us even in these modern days." Yes, but also something repellent, anarchic, almost frightening. Transcendental freedom, their laughter seems to say, is no joke.

Do the Oriental hermit-sage-poets of old, lonely and rootless, innocent and childish, wise with a wisdom they themselves call foolish, neither listening to reason nor, with any consistency, speaking it, have anything to say to us of the wired world?

The divergence between our ways and theirs goes back very far, at least two and a half millennia, to the time of the archetypal world-renouncing hermit-sage Lao-tzu. He lived in China in the sixth century BC, roughly a century before the Athenian statesman Pericles, with whom a comparison is instructive. How does Lao-tzu describe himself? "Possibly mine is the mind of a fool, which is so ignorant!... I alone seem to be dull... I alone seem to be blunt... I alone seem to be impractical and awkward..."

Pericles would have given all this very short shrift. He had no time for ignorance and awkwardness, and a famous line from his Funeral Oration can almost be read as a sharp retort to the sage's babble: "Here [in Athens] each individual is interested not only in his own affairs but in the affairs of the state as well... We do not say that a man who takes no interest in politics is a man who minds his own business; we say that he has no business here at all."

Wherein, we might well ask, lies Lao-tzu's sagacity? In his being "like a baby who is yet unable to smile?" Yes, and in this: "I value seeking sustenance from the Mother" – that is, the Tao, the Way. And what is the Way, and where does it take us? "Those who know do not speak," goes the celebrated reply. "Those who speak do not know."

Imagine the ancient Athenians not speaking their wisdom! They would have choked on it, for what was wisdom if not fuel for speech, and what was speech if not the very best thing in life, the activity a wise man was born for, the medium that linked him to his fellows in the united search for a universal truth, as true for me as for you, as true today as two thousand years ago?

Knowledge that cannot be spoken, however nourishing to the inner life, poses special challenges to social intercourse. It encourages reclusion at the expense of assembly. The Oriental distrust of speech is as widespread as it is ancient, and as deeply rooted as is the Occidental fondness for it. The Buddha, roughly contemporaneous with Lao Tzu, included Right Speech in his Eightfold Path to Enlightenment, and his meaning, explains the eminent modern scholar Christmas Humphreys, was that "All idle gossip and unprofitable talk must be stamped out. Silence should be so respected that the words which break it must leave the world the better for their birth." Thus admonished, a man might well hesitate to open his mouth. "I may not have made any special vow of silence," remarked the twelfth-century Japanese recluse Kamo no Chomei, "but as I am all alone I am little likely to offend with the tongue."

Even teachers preferred silence to words, for the highest wisdom was not, as in the West, shared knowledge of the outer world but an intensely private, individual, incommunicable intuition. The student came seeking not information but liberation – from the conceptualization, first of all, which language by its very nature forces on us.

"How silent! How solitary!" said Lao-tzu of the Tao and its seekers. The Buddha concurred. "Buddhas do but point the way," he said. "Work out your own salvation with diligence."

What islands of solitary contemplation the mountain mists of Japan once veiled!

The classic example is Kamo no Chomei's "ten-foot-square hut." Discouraged by career setbacks and dizzied by the senseless flux and motion of the world, he spent the final decades of his life in secluded mountain retirement. A ravaging fire and a devastating earthquake taught him early in life what can be expected from this most evanescent and capricious of worlds. Natural disasters aside, is this world, with its greed, its envy, its lack of sympathy, really a place a decent man can live in?

Surely not, he decided, and withdrew, first to a lonely shack by a riverbed, and then, thirty years later, to the mountains, to a series of rustic huts, each smaller than the last. With old age approaching, he began to jot down his thoughts. They are serene, contented, resigned:

"In this impermanent hut of mine all is calm and there is nothing to fear."

"Like a drifting cloud I rely on no one and have no attachments."

"I commit my life to fate without special wish to live or desire to die."

His final reflection is that he has not after all fully renounced his worldly ties, for he cannot altogether overcome his affection for his little thatched hut, and "my attachment to this solitary life," however threadbare, "may be a hindrance to enlightenment." In a similar vein the priest Kenko no Yoshida (c.1283-c.1350) refers in *The Grasses of Idleness* to "a certain hermit" who said, "There is one thing that even I, who have no worldly entanglements, would be sorry to give up, the beauty of the sky." Chomei's contemporary, the poet Saigyo

98

(1118-90) found himself no less ensnared by the beauty of the moon.

What does a person learn, cut off from the society of his fellows and numb to the attractions of the only world our senses can know? What do solitude and detachment teach us? Foolishness? Ryokan and Lao-tzu both claimed foolishness as an attribute, Lao-tzu explicitly seeing in it a higher wisdom. Perhaps we were wrong to banish it from our scheme of things. Suzuki's name for foolishness is "purposelessness," which to him is a prerequisite, if not an actual synonym, for freedom. Dedicated as we today tend to be to the pursuit of this or that goal in life, we fool ourselves in calling ourselves free, though undoubtedly we are busy. Ryokan, beggar, idler, self-described "lazy old horse," sings this paean to perfect freedom:

If anyone asks
say I'm in the grove
of Otogo Shrine
picking up fallen leaves under the trees

And if no one asks, an unspoken corollary seems to whisper, that's fine too.

Rags and tatters, rags and tatters
rags and tatters – that's my life.
Food – somehow I pick it up along the road;
my house – I let the weeds grow all around.
Watching the moon, I spend the whole night
mumbling poems.
Lost in blossoms, I never come home.

Ryokan "left the world" at seventeen. Eldest son of a village headman in Echigo province, today's Niigata Prefecture, he abruptly entered a Zen temple, turning his back on his presumed future as his father's successor.

Status, respect, prosperity – all were his; all he had to do was grow into them. No, he said. Why? No one knows.

> *It's not that*
> *I never mix*
> *with men of the world –*
> *but really, I'd rather amuse myself alone*

Is that an explanation? Did he have an intimation that a higher destiny awaited him? If so, what was it?

> *I've forgotten my begging bowl*
> *but no one would steal it*
> *no one would steal it*
> *how sad for my begging bowl!*

And how happy for him.

> *Children!*
> *shall we be going now*
> *to the hill of Iyahiko*
> *to see how the violets are blooming?*

His long life, in its externals, is easily summarized: he wandered, lived alone in temples and one-room huts, begged for food, was often hungry, adored children (being scarcely more than a child himself), loved all living things, down to the lice in his rags and tatters, and wrote poetry. What did he have to show for it at the end?

Dysentery – and the means to celebrate even that in verse:

With these runny bowels
my body is hard to bear!

"If one knows himself and knows what the world is," mused Kamo no Chomei in the solitude of his ten-foot-square hut nearly a thousand years ago, "he will merely wish for quiet and be pleased when he has nothing to grieve about, wanting nothing and caring for nobody." That makes us smile. We consider we know a lot more about the world and how it works than Kamo did, and one thing we know is that wanting nothing is no way to cure a sick economy, ailing precisely because of its failure to make us want enough. Moreover, happiness defined as the absence of grief no longer attracts us. For us happiness is a pursuit, the more active the better. We have remade the world in our modern image: it pulses and throbs with our energy.

Have we outgrown the recluses of old? Are we too rational for their inspired nonsense, too sober for their lunatic laughter, too full for their hungry joy, too firmly wired and webbed for their anarchic solitude?

One day in 1924, a time in many ways analogous to ours because Japan's first compulsive modernization drive was at roughly the stage its second one is at today, a middle-aged drunk staggering across a Kumamoto street came within inches of being run over by a trolley. An annoyed passenger leapt off the trolley, collared the fool, and dragged him off to a nearby Zen temple for discipline and reflection. The passenger had no way of knowing who he was dealing with, or that his initiative

101

would have deep consequences. The fool in question was the haiku poet Taneda Santoka – chronic wanderer, chronic drunk, chronic scribbler of such lines as

> *Parting from my brother*
> *never to meet him again*
> *I tramp the muddy road.*

His brother had recently committed suicide, as had his mother years earlier. At the temple he absorbed Buddhist teachings and took the tonsure. Begging bowl in hand, he resumed his way, bound for that best of all places, if only we can find it – nowhere.

> *The road on which I've lost my way*
> *is where I'll spend the night.*

He died in a hermitage in 1940, and was soon forgotten. What does his rediscovery in the 1970s and his enduring popularity today tell us? That Emptiness leaves a void when it is cast out by excessive plenitude?

"Let neither of us think too much," Santoka once wrote to a friend. "Let us become more foolish. Better: let us revert to our original foolishness."

Why choose foolishness? What can foolishness give us that intelligence leaves us lacking? Ryokan, the Great Fool, has an answer:

> *Wonderful, the mood of this moment –*
> *distant, vast, known to me only!*

(2001)

Death, I Love You

ONE MARCH MORNING in 1999 an undistinguished Bridgestone Tire executive strode into the company president's office and did something obsolete. He had come, he said, to protest the rigorous staff reduction policy that was costing thousands of middle managers like himself their jobs. Did the president not realize the anguish this was causing? Did the victims' decades of loyal, devoted service to the company mean nothing? Wrapping up an hour-long harangue, the fifty-eight-year-old man stripped down to his underwear and drew two 35-cm knives from his attaché case. "Will you change the current personnel policy?" he demanded. Impossible, the president replied. "In that case," said the executive, "I will cut my belly open and die." He paused. "Let us die together." Without waiting for an answer, he plunged a knife into his abdomen.

Osaka, 1703. Tokubei loves Ohatsu, Ohatsu loves Tokubei. He deals in soy sauce. She is a prostitute. Ah, if only the world wasn't so complicated! If only the human heart wasn't so crooked! Tokubei has no money, and is a simpleton besides, a perfect pigeon in the hands of the artful schemers who surround him. A penniless man has no easy access to the prostitute he loves. Ohatsu comforts him: "And if a time should come when we can no longer met, did our promises of love hold only for this world? Others before us have chosen reunion through death." So be it. "Farewell to the world, and to the night farewell!" Their midnight dash to freedom ends in a wood; he stabs her in the throat and cuts his own throat with a razor, and they draw their last rattling breaths together, "models of true love." So indeed they must have seemed to contemporary audiences, judging by the number of lovers who, apparently following their example, rushed to end their own lives in each other's arms.

A modern reader of Chikamatsu – for Chikamatsu is the playwright, dramatizing an episode that had actually occurred only a month before his play opened – might wonder why he did not have his lovers consummate their death vows. The limitations of his medium no doubt counted for something – he wrote for the puppet theater. Or perhaps carnal love is simply beside the point when the union of souls is at issue. Be that as it may, it was left to the modern writer Yukio Mishima to explore the eros of death in all its awful glory. The story in which he does so most explicitly is titled *Patriotism*, and to the reader who does not share Mishima's unusual psychology it is one of the ghastliest visions in all literature. The story takes place on February 28, 1936. A murderous revolt by junior army officers intent on restoring power to the Emperor has been crushed, and Lieutenant Takeyama, who was not included in the mutiny owing to his recent marriage, is resolved to kill himself in sympathy with his comrades. His new bride does not hesitate. She will follow her husband in death. "With happiness welling almost too abundantly in their hearts, they could not help smiling at each other. Reiko felt as if she had returned to her wedding night."

The couple bathe, drink saké and, dizzy with passion, the passion of impending young death, make love. "Gazing at the youthful, firm stomach, modestly covered by a vigorous growth of hair, Reiko thought of it as it was soon to be, cruelly cut by the sword, and she laid her head upon it, sobbing in pity, and bathed it with kisses.

"At the touch of his wife's tears upon his stomach the lieutenant felt ready to endure with courage the cruelest agonies of suicide.

"What ecstasies they experienced after these tender exchanges may well be imagined." That being the case we say no more, though Mishima's eloquence was far from exhausted. Death, to him, is the ultimate orgasm. He sought it all his life. In the end, as the world knows, he found it.

Birth and death we share with the animals: awe is ours alone. The shaped tools generally cited as our first purely human achievement accompanied another development, perhaps even more distinctively human: ceremonial burial. A Neanderthal grave found in northern Iraq had been strewn with wildflowers. We'll never know what thoughts and feelings animated the mourners who gathered them. But we can sense in these proto-humans assembled round a grave some mental ferment, together with the urge to express it. Death: man's first art.

And life's supreme mystery – as obscure as ever after millennia of civilization and centuries of science.

We can describe the Big Bang, plot the course of the remotest stars, trace the evolution of life back to the primeval slime, and map the human genome. But of what awaits us after death we are as ignorant, scientifically speaking, as our most savage forebears. Odder yet, we are somewhat reconciled to our ignorance – as our forebears were not, and as we ourselves are in no other domain. Death is one barrier most of us today prefer not to cross before we have to, and science, not as a rule gracious about acknowledging closed paths, does acknowledge this one. No one is proposing an equivalent of the space program for the land of the dead. Ancient and medieval explorers – Odysseus, St. Hildegaard, Dante – have no modern counterparts.

It was Socrates who said it is stupid to fear death. Why recoil from what we know nothing about? Why assume it's an evil? Maybe it's a blessing. Maybe good men – that is, men who have devoted their lives to philosophy – will find after death the home their souls have yearned for since being yoked at birth to a physical body. The notion had a long future ahead of it, in the somewhat modified form of the Christian heaven.

If death is a mystery, unknown and unknowable, we are of course free to deck it in whatever colors we choose, and since (so large does it loom) we cannot help thinking about it, the combination of total ignorance, unfettered imagination and (Socrates notwithstanding) instinctive fear is bound to generate an infinity of visions of what awaits us on the other shore. Heaven, hell, Hades, Nirvana, Samsara, nothingness – if we want to see human inventiveness at work unbounded by even the smallest hard fact, we can do no better than study its response to the challenge of death.

To the wealth of ecstatic phantasms that resulted, the Japanese have contributed little. The vague horror of death characteristic of early Shinto begot nothing like Odysseus' gibbering shades flitting about in eternal night, or St. Hildegaard's souls writhing in wells of boiling pitch. Nor do the splendors of Amida Buddha's Pure Land – a splendid resort but nothing more – approach the infinite and ineffable bliss of the Christian Paradise. The real Japanese theater of death is neither the starry heavens nor the fiery pits of hell. It is right here, the drama unfolding on the very stage where we lead our lives. Not since ancient Egypt has death been so immediate, so intimate, one is almost tempted to say so cherished a presence (is not the cherry blossom one of its main symbols?) as it is, and has long been, in Japan. No aspect of Japanese life can be discussed without reference to death: love, art, beauty, business (in 1982 the American newsweekly *Time* quoted with bemusement rule number 7 of a certain Osaka tent manufacturer's 12-item company credo: "Once you've grabbed hold of a potential piece of business, never let it go – even at risk of your own life"), war (well, naturally – and yet one has only to mention the kamikaze pilots of World War Two to suggest a difference in degree so sharp as to amount to a difference in kind), dignity (almost synonymous with and, in a tradition that endures to this day, instantly acquirable by a demonstrated willingness to die) and religion (how characteristic that Buddhism, the most benign and least bellicose of all religions, should in Japan have nurtured a branch called Zen, among whose emblems is the murderous 'sword of life' and among whose mottos is, 'If you are really desirous of mastering Zen, it is necessary to give up your life and plunge right into the pit of death.'')

"Death," wrote Hideo Kishimoto in *The Japanese Mind* (1967), "is not a mere end of life for the Japanese. It has been given a positive place in life. Facing death properly is one of the most important features of life. In that sense it may well be said that for the Japanese, death is within life."

Japan's first purely human – that is, non-mythological – hero is a warrior named Yorozu. He lived in the sixth century. He battled the enemy against hopeless odds until, having exhausted his supply of arrows, he stabbed himself in the throat to avoid capture. The respectful treatment accorded him in the eighth-century *Nihon Shoki* is remarkable – he fought on the losing side, and the chronicle was written by the winners. The clash was between two leading clans, one favoring the adoption of Buddhism, the other defending the native Shinto cult. Buddhism won, and though Shinto didn't exactly lose (a very long future lay ahead of it) the clan championing the native religion's exclusive rights over the Japanese soul was soundly defeated, its only lasting contribution to history being the dead body of Yorozu. Thus centuries before Zen, centuries before the Way of the Warrior, the peculiarly Japanese approach to war and death is delineated. A warrior's life, and his cause, pale in comparison to the manner of his death. More than right, more than justice, more than wealth, more than victory, a beautiful death came to be the warrior's goal. Refinement came with the passage of time. Hara-kiri or *seppuku*, the excruciating ritual of disembowelment that further sets the Japanese warrior apart from his fellows elsewhere, seems an innovation of

108

the eleventh century, an apparent by-product of the notion that the spirit resides in the belly.

"I cannot believe in Western sincerity," Mishima told a foreign correspondent four years before his own seppuku, "because it is invisible, but in feudal times we believed that sincerity resided in our entrails, and if we needed to show our sincerity, we had to cut our bellies and take out our *visible* sincerity." How ironic that his own death should have partaken of such a theatrical flavor!

Japan's greatest tea master is reputedly Sen no Rikyu, who lived during the turbulent sixteenth century and was an intimate friend of one of that century's most dangerous and powerful men, Toyotomi Hideyoshi. This is a strange and bumptious companion for the man to whom we owe some of the subtlest nuances of *wabi* and *sabi* – meaning, broadly speaking, the wealth of poverty and the intimacy of loneliness. The tea ceremony he elaborated to embody these elusive qualities is exquisitely detailed, though punctuated by a touch of whimsy, as we sense, for example, in his irritation over his son's having swept the tearoom courtyard too clean. "Young fool," he said, "that is not the way a garden path should be swept!" – whereupon he shook a tree until enough leaves had fallen to produce the desired effect. He was seventy when he committed seppuku, on orders from Hideyoshi, who was offended, according to one of several conflicting accounts, by a statue of Rikyu so situated that the warlord was obliged to walk beneath the teaman's feet. Very well, said Rikyu. He hosted a farewell tea party, composed a death poem, and, to borrow Mishima's expression, showed his sincerity.

Is it surprising that a life of tea should prepare a man to die calmly on command? Rikyu was, like most great Japanese artists, a student of Zen, which taught the art of living in "a realm beyond birth and death" – as did Socrates, who said that the essence of philosophy was learning how to die. Socrates and Rikyu make for an interesting comparison. Both were seventy when they died, both were victims of injustice, and both died bravely. The similarities are striking; the differences more so. Socrates stood trial, was accorded due process; he would never have committed suicide on an enraged tyrant's order; nor, perhaps, would he have seen Rikyu's serene acquiescence as noble. As for Rikyu, one can hardly imagine him spending his last hours in intense discussion on the nature of the soul and its fate after death. Rikyu, like Socrates, died surrounded by his friends – but instead of philosophizing he held a tea party. Instead of conducting a discourse, he composed a poem:

Welcome to thee
o sword of eternity!...

In Japan, greatness goes hand in hand with poetry. "A feeling for poetry," wrote the historian Ivan Morris, "was a confirmation of the warrior's sincerity." Nowhere is the Japanese view of death as art more evident than in the custom of inditing a death verse. One might suppose a man at such a moment would be too agitated to attend to the whisper of the poetic muse. Not so. "Death is the most serious affair, absorbing all one's attention," said Zen master Daisetz T. Suzuki, "but cultured Japanese

110

think they ought to be able to transcend it and view it objectively."

Fervent poets all were the kamikaze airmen, the human bombs of World War Two.

If only we might fall
like cherry blossoms in spring
so pure and radiant!

May our deaths be as sudden and clean
as the shattering of crystal!

Such were the sentiments that drove them.

The kamikaze sorties were the brainchild of Vice Admiral Takijiro Onishi, the Navy's top airman in the Philippines. This is no blustering militarist bully but a highly sensitive, deeply conflicted man – and a poet. On August 15, 1945, at midnight, he committed seppuku. He took hours to die. His death poem:

Refreshed and clear
the moon now shines
after the fearful storm.

Warriors in other countries die too, of course, and die bravely, but they die for the most part in the belief that it is better to live, and that dying represents a sacrifice, necessary perhaps but unfortunate. The Japanese attitude is different. In place of the Judeo-Christian notion – violated often enough but never entirely lost from sight – that life is a gift, the Japanese have another notion, no less deeply embedded: that of impermanence. Flowers fade, cherry blossoms fall. This evanescence is not just a regrettable peripheral property of these beautiful things. It is the essence of their beauty. Blossoms are not beautiful in spite of their transience. They are beautiful *because* they are transient. This is why a kamikaze pilot with less than a day left to live could write home: "Dear Parents, please congratulate me. I have been given a splendid opportunity to die." And it is why Mishima could not see a beautiful body without immediately being put in mind of death. Sickly and weak as a youth, by sheer force of will he sculpted his own body into a splendid vessel – a vessel worthy of the death he had conceived for it.

The courtship of death spread outward from the samurai class. Mishima might have been a kind of pseudo-samurai, but what of his bohemian fellow-novelist Osamu Dazai? (They are two of at least ten major twentieth-century Japanese writer who died by their own hands.) Opposite in nearly every way – Dazai the tubercular drug addict cultivated his weakness as assiduously as Mishima the bodybuilder cultivated his strength – they nonetheless shared an infatuation with death, and Mishima, though he affected a lofty disdain for the older writer, nonetheless wrote of him, "What I despise about Dazai is that he exposes precisely those things in myself I most want to hide."

Mishima laid siege to death; Dazai flirted coyly with it. His fifth suicide attempt was successful – he and a lover drowned themselves in the Tamagawa Canal. It was second-rate Chikamatsu, just as Mishima's death was second-rate Mishima, pathetically inferior to the death of his own hero, Lieutenant Takeyama.

Prominent in Japan's modern heroic pantheon is Saigo Takamori, the giant of a man whose statue towers over strollers and picnickers at Tokyo's Ueno Park. Like Yorozu centuries earlier, he was a reactionary, a historical footnote who killed himself defending the past against the future. Also like Yorozu, he was immortalized by the victorious enemy – immortalized not for his accomplishments or his ideas but for the manner of his death. Saigo's politics were actually more complex – more psychological – than the blunt word "reactionary" suggests. Born into a low-ranking samurai family in Kagoshima, he helped lead the Meiji Restoration of 1868, only to turn against it later in indignation over the wholesale adoption of Western materialism. The Satsuma rebellion of 1872 pitted his disaffected samurai followers against Japan's first conscript army, whose crushing victory was a final nail in the coffin of the samurai ethos. Naturally, Saigo was a poet. Quitting the government in disgust when his plan to invade Korea was vetoed, he wrote, "I have shaken off the dust of this world." In rustic retirement at home in Kyushu, he sketched a philosophy of death: "One must clearly understand that life and death are not two things... Since the true home of our spirits is outside both life and death, what have we to fear?" This is more resonant to a Japanese mind than to a Western, though Socrates might have nodded in thoughtful sympathy.

No soldier better typifies the life spent in pursuit of death. There are echoes of both Mishima and Dazai here. A failed attempt at age thirty to drown himself haunted him all his life – the Shinto priest who was to be his companion in death was successful, leaving Saigo alone and abandoned in the world of the living. Ivan Morris

113

regarded the thwarted Korean invasion as no more than an elaborate suicide plan. "Sometimes," he remarked, "it must have seemed to Saigo that death was deliberately evading him."

Japan today, ironically, is the longest-living nation on earth. Medical advances and social drift have conspired to keep people alive long past a point where society knows what to do with them. Death evades us still, only now the issue is not "beautiful death" but death with dignity. The nation that practically invented the former lags behind in the latter. The initiatives are coming instead from nations like the Netherlands, which in 2001 became the first to legalize euthanasia.

Japan's courtship of death persists all the same. In 1998 the number of suicides – 30,000 plus – was extreme enough to cause a measurable decline, 0.21 percent, in male life expectancy. Economic despair is the explanation most commonly invoked. Seppuku figures rarely in modern suicide. The lifelong education in the Way of the Warrior that is prerequisite to such excruciating self-slaughter is no longer provided, and the mass ridicule heaped upon Mishima's gutted body is no doubt a further discouragement. Most people today die as quietly as they live. The Bridgestone executive was an exception, but a revealing one. He chose to die in the manner of his country's heroes. Barred from the future, he cast his lot with the past, when all failure was gloriously redeemable with a knife and a naked belly.

(2001)

"Just So, Subhuti": Zen All, Zen Nothing

"Just so, Subhuti, I obtained not the least thing from unexcelled, complete awakening, and for this very reason it is called 'unexcelled, complete awakening'!"

THE FIRST THING TO APPRECIATE about Zen is that it's easy. The second thing to appreciate is that it's incomprehensible. A contradiction? Only if you insist on trying to understand. To be enlightened is to resign yourself to – no, to delight in – incomprehension.

A story: Seeing some monks under his tutelage fighting over a cat, the Chinese Zen Master Nansen (748-834) snatched the cat and said, "Say something or I'll cut it in two!" The monks gaped, speechless. Nansen cut the cat. Later, he told his disciple Joshu what had happened. Joshu immediately took off his sandals, put them on his head and walked out. "If you had been there," said Nansen, "you would have saved the cat."

Japanese Zen is Chinese Taoism blended with Indian mysticism, steeped in Confucian and samurai discipline, then spiced with a faint but unmistakable hint of madness. Its heart is vagrant, its mind vacant, its belly hungry.

The prototypical Zen-man is Lao-tzu, who in the sixth century BC, a millennium before Zen was ever heard of, wrote with pride in the *Tao Te Ching* of his foolishness, forlornness, impracticality and disinclination to attach himself to anything. His redeeming virtue is his willingness to "seek sustenance from the Mother" – the Tao, the Way. Here Zen acolytes too have sought sustenance, since the semi-legendary Indian patriarch Bodhidarma introduced meditation to Chinese seekers in the sixth century AD.

Bodhidarma's famous Japanese incarnation is the roly-poly legless Daruma doll – legless because the master, so it is said, sat so long in meditation that his legs withered. A Chinese acolyte, desperate to distract him long enough to receive his advice, cut off his own arm as a token of his sincerity. "Very well," sighed Bodhidarma at last. "What can I do for you?"

"I have no peace of mind," said the acolyte. "Please pacify my mind."

"Give me your mind," replied Bodhidarma, "and I will pacify it."

"But when I seek my mind," said the acolyte, "I cannot find it."

"Well, there you are!" said Bodhidarma, "I have pacified your mind!"

It's a characteristic Zen story – razor-sharp, funny, perfectly lucid and at the same time totally bewildering. It's typical in another way too: it induced in the acolyte the mysterious instant awakening – satori – which is Zen's most distinctive feature.

Three core principles comprise Zen. The first, held in common with other forms of Buddhism, is

116

non-existence. The second is the utter uselessness – worse, the utter destructiveness – of trying to intellectually comprehend Reality. The third is the capacity of intuition to effortlessly succeed where intellect fails. The catch is that intuition cannot be communicated. Thus the famous Zen proverb, "Those who know don't speak" – and vice versa.

If "I" is an abstraction, why do we so keenly feel our "I-ness"? René Descartes, the seventeenth-century thinker and mathematician generally regarded as the father of modern philosophy, found he could doubt everything except his own existence. Zen not only doubts our existence, it categorically denies it. "All things," writes Hosshinji Temple Abbot Sekkei Harada in *The Essence of Zen*, "are transient. All things are without self. All things are in the peace and tranquility of Nirvana."

If only we knew it! Deluded by the illusion of selfhood, of individual separation form the True Self that is the cosmos, we miss what would otherwise be perfectly plain. Nirvana is here, now. We are undone by our tendency to seek it far away and in the future – to seek it, period. The consequences are devastating. "To think there is a self when in fact there isn't," writes Harada, "is ignorance. To perceive the self, then, is evil. It is a complete hindrance to the practice of the Way."

Western civilization since Descartes has been based on the ego-self, the rigid separation of "I" from "not-I" – and, increasingly, the relentless gratification of the former at the expense, if necessary, of the latter. Brought up as egos, we are inclined to regard egotism as natural, and egolessness as just another mystic Oriental notion that makes no sense. That it makes no sense is true. Where Zen and more formal systems of thought part company is in Zen's acceptance – its *joyous* acceptance – of senselessness.

117

"It is a great mistake," argues Daisetz T. Suzuki in *Zen and Japanese Culture*, "to adjust everything to the Procrustean bed of logic, and a greater mistake to make logic the supreme test in the evaluation of human behavior." Let logic, he says, adapt itself to life, freeing life from the distorting obligation to adapt to logic. Only then can we be what the ancient Chinese master Te-shan would have us be: "Vacant and spiritual, empty and marvelous."

"East is East and West is West," said Kipling – untruly, as we now know, having over the past half-century watched the twain meet and merge. But he, rooted in another time, had observed real differences. Broadly speaking, the classical East saw the universe as chaos that grew, while the West saw it as order that had been created; the East approached the world as children at a playground, the West as workers in a factory; the East emphasized poetry, the West science.

Zen has been called "the very heart of Asian spirituality," inaccessible to the Western mind because logic-bound Western thinkers, not satisfied with "the world in its such-ness," uncomfortable with "the total elusiveness of the world," insists on taking intellectual hold of reality and forcing it into a mold called "sense."

Wonderful, the mood of this moment
distant, vast, known to me only!

Thus the poet Ryokan (1758-1831) summed up the fruits of the Zen life. Hermit, monk, beggar, eternal child, he is one of a long line of unfettered personalities who make us wish we could all be Zen-men. Suzuki tells of him unwittingly setting fire to his hut while trying to burn a hole in his roof for a bamboo shoot to grow through. Idiot! Fool! Lunatic! But read his poetry. You can't help thinking, as you do, that he knew something about life that more worldly people miss.

Living without self, exclusively in the moment, has its moral hazards. Think of Nansen and the cat – does anyone pause to pity the poor cat? Apparently not.

Think also of Zen's militarist tradition. The sword wielded by a Zen-trained swordsman is not, we are told, the sword that kills but the sword that gives life. It requires a peculiarly unskeptical cast of mind to take that on faith. "Those who cling to life die, those who defy death live," said the sixteenth-century warrior Uesugi Kenshin. Daiun Sogaku Harada was a twentieth-century Zen master, Sekkei Harada's predecessor as abbot of Hosshinji, and no warrior. Yet in 1939, with Japanese militarism at its height, he wrote, "[If ordered to] march: tramp, tramp; or to shoot: bang, bang. This is the manifestation of the highest [enlightened] wisdom."

It may be so, in which case either "tramp, tramp, bang, bang" represents humanity at its best, or else Zen enlightenment is a most uncertain path to a better world. After all, wordless, illogical wisdom will naturally shape itself to the character of the person claiming it. In the hands of a Harada, it's "tramp, tramp, bang, bang." In the hands of a Ryokan?

Taking my time I go begging for food – how wide, how boundless this Dharma world!

(2002)

119

The Christian Century

SOME SCHOLARS SAY Japan's Christian history began long before the "Christian century" (1549-c.1640). Their claim takes us all the way back to seventh- and eighth-century Nara, where Nestorian Christians from Persia are said to have built churches, operated a leper hospital and even converted the Empress Komyo, wife of the devout Buddhist Emperor Shomu (reigned 724-749), to Christianity.

The evidence is tantalizing but inconclusive. If they existed, Nara's Christians left no mark on the culture. Spanish and Portuguese Jesuit missionaries who arrived some eight hundred years later not only had to start from scratch, they had to *define* scratch. How to begin to explain, across a towering language barrier, such alien and mysterious concepts as the Virgin Birth, the sacrifice on the Cross of the Son of God for the redemption of mankind?

The scale of the task is a measure of the determination of the men who faced it, and Francis Xavier, the Basque Jesuit whose landing at Kagoshima in August 1549 inaugurates the "Christian century," was nothing if not determined.

A prayer attributed to him begins, "Eternal God, Creator of all things, remember that the souls of unbelievers have been created by thee and formed to thine own image and likeness. Behold, O Lord, how to thy dishonor hell is being filled with these very souls...

Do not permit, O Lord, I beseech thee, that thy divine Son be any longer despised by unbelievers…"

Thus fortified, the future saint went to work on the Japanese.

Xavier had by then been in Asia seven years. He arrived in Goa, "the Rome of India," capital of Portugal's Far Eastern empire, in 1542. He traveled vast distances, much of his missionary work unfolding among cannibals and warriors of remote South Asian islands.

In 1547 he was on his way back to Goa when he heard at Malacca encouraging reports of a new Asian discovery. Four years earlier some Portuguese traders blown off course by a storm had been the first Europeans known to set foot in Japan. "There," wrote Xavier, "according to the Portuguese, much fruit might be gained for the increase of our holy faith, more than in any other part of the Indies, for they are a people most desirous of knowledge, which the Indian heathen are not."

At Malacca he met a Japanese, a sometime pirate named Yajiro. "He came to seek me with a great desire to know about our religion." Yajiro, christened Paul, became Xavier's companion and interpreter. He proved a mixed blessing.

Japan in the sixteenth century was disintegrating. Feudal lord fought feudal lord; combat had become epidemic. "There was not a province in Japan," writes the historian George Sansom, "free from the armed rivalry of territorial barons or lords of the [Buddhist] church." Few in 1549 would have foreseen the solidly united nation that was to emerge a scant fifty years later.

Nor was there much in Xavier's first faltering steps in this unknown land to suggest the groundswell of success soon to reward the Jesuits' unshakable confidence and dedication. The success was brilliant but fleeting. It ended tragically in what Engelbert Kaempfer, a German physician and chronicler stationed at Nagasaki early in the eighteenth century, called "the most cruel persecution and torture of Christians ever witnessed on this globe... lasting more than forty yeas until the last drop of Christian blood was spilled."

Xavier, Yajiro and two Jesuit companions boarded a pirate ship at Malacca and disembarked at Kagoshima in southern Kyushu. Xavier was impatient to push on to Kyoto and convert "the king of Japan." The trouble was, there *was* no "king of Japan," only an emperor who was powerless and a shogun, Ashikaga Yoshiteru, who was even more so. Central authority had broken down. The bringers of the Word would have to be content to deal with warlords – who were, for the most part, accommodating. The Kyushu and southern Honshu daimyo were quick to see the value of Portuguese backing, Portuguese trade and, of course, Portuguese guns, first introduced into Japanese warfare around this time. If a courteous reception of the missionaries brought such rewards, it seemed a small price to pay.

Xavier and his little band were first welcomed at Kagoshima by the "king of Satsuma" – the daimyo Shimazu Takehisa. He granted them permission to preach in the streets, and listened to them dispute the finer points of ultimate reality with a group of Zen monks. Yajiro's skills as an interpreter, which modern scholars do not rate highly, must have been taxed to the limit. Still, the mutual goodwill among the parties was such that the missionaries were deeply distressed when the monks declined baptism – "preferring," lamented the contemporary Jesuit chronicler Luis Frois, "to land lost and miserable in hell."

The padres did better on the streets, baptizing, according to Frois, one hundred fifty people in the ten months they were there.

Yamaguchi in southern Honshu was their next stop, and there too the "king" was cordial, at least at first. His sudden change of mood suggests the thin ice the missionaries trod. Here is Sansom's account: "Xavier had an audience with [the daimyo Ouchi Yoshitaka], at whose request he told the interpreter to read in Japanese a document, already prepared, which gave the elements of Christian doctrine. This included a discourse upon error and sin. When the reader came to a passage on sodomy, describing those guilty of this offense as filthier than swine and lower than dogs, the daimyo changed color and dismissed them, no doubt because he, in common with many military men in that part of Japan, was given to such habits. The interpreter thought they might have their heads cut off, but they left safely."

As in Kagoshima, Xavier in Yamaguchi got on well with the Buddhist priests. Here the prevailing sect was Shingon, which worships the Buddha Vairocana, Dainichi in Japanese. A befuddled Yajiro convinced Xavier that Dainichi was none other than the Christian "Deus-sama" in oriental dress, that Shingon and Christianity were essentially one.

This was good news indeed, but it did not bear scrutiny. "[Xavier] approached the monks again," writes Sansom, "and questioned them on the mystery of the Holy Trinity, asking whether they believed the second Person of the Trinity had become a man and had died on the cross to save mankind. The Shingon monks were accustomed to mysteries, but these things were so strange to them that they seemed like fables or dreams, and some laughed at what the father said."

Realizing his mistake, Xavier turned acerbic. He now taught, says Frois, that Shingon was "an invention of the devil, as also were all the other sects of Japan."

Xavier left Japan in 1551, strangely enough more hopeful than discouraged. Stranger still, his hope was borne out – for a time; a very brief time.

On July 24, 1587, Toyotomi Hideyoshi, the second of the thee great unifiers of Japan and by then Japan's most powerful warlord – issued an edict giving the foreign purveyors of the "pernicious doctrine" twenty days to leave the country.

It was a bolt out of the blue. Christianity's prospects had flowered splendidly in the thirty-six years since Xavier's departure. By 1582 there were two hundred churches serving an estimated 150,000 native Christians. Common people aside, the Jesuits had friends and allies in high places, none friendlier or higher than Hideyoshi himself, or so it seemed. Had he not, in 1586, granted the padres the right to reside and preach the gospel unmolested "in all the lands of Japan"?

Here and there, though not everywhere, Christianity was starting to look like the wave of the future. Omura Sumitada, lord of the territory surrounding Nagasaki, became Japan's first Christian daimyo, receiving baptism in 1563 and being given the Christian name Bartholomeu. Eleven years later, beset by regional enemies, he was extricated by a Portuguese fleet – in return for which, suggested the Jesuit Gaspar Coelho, Bartholomeu ought, as the chronicler Frois records, to "extinguish totally the

125

worship and veneration of idols in his lands" until "not a single pagan remained."

The result was Japan's first forcible mass conversion. Buddhist temples and Shinto shrines were burned to the ground, and Christianity at one stroke gained sixty thousand new converts. (A similar if less violent mass conversion was imposed in 1577 on the nearby Shimabara Peninsula. It bore tragic fruit six decades later, as we shall see.)

To the east of Bartolomeu's domain lay the province of Bungo, whose daimyo, Otomo Sorin, had been well-disposed towards the Portuguese since Xavier's passage through his territory in 1551. His lively protestations, in letters to the Portuguese base at Macao, of respect for "the things of God" and "the Christians who are in my kingdom" accompany requests for arms, making it difficult to ascertain which side of the spiritual-temporal divide was uppermost in his mind. On the one hand, he did not accept baptism until 1578; on the other hand, having accepted it, he seems to have embraced the new faith wholeheartedly. History knows him best as "Good King Francisco" – and his wife, deeply and (so it is said) shrewishly anti-Christian, as "Jezebel."

Like his neighbor Bartolomeu, Good King Francisco indulged a passion for temple- and shrine-burning – most notably in a neighboring province he invaded in May 1578, intending, Frois tells us, to turn it into a model Christian community.

Alas, the victory proved short-lived. The defeated enemy rallied and Francisco fled back to Bungo – evidence, to Frois, of God's wish to "punish the people of Bungo" for sins which "had accumulated to an extent that God could no longer ignore."

Hideyoshi's abrupt expulsion order opens the final act of the drama of the "Christian century." Mildly enforced at first, it culminated in the relentless torture and persecution Kaempfer speaks of, an agonizing, appalling, ultimately futile mass martyrdom whose most obvious parallel is a supremely ironic one – the martyrdom the Catholic Inquisitions were at that very time inflicting on "heretics" in Europe.

For ten years there were few signs that Hideyoshi meant business. Missionary activity and Christian worship carried on much as before, officials looking on tolerantly as new converts were brought daily into the fold.

In 1596 Hideyoshi had only two years left to live. Might history have been different had the pilot of a Spanish galleon from the Philippines not in that year boasted of the power of the Spanish Empire, and of the missionaries who pave the way for its overseas conquests?

Thus provoked, Hideyoshi acted swiftly. On February 5, 1597 in Nagasaki, twenty-six Christians – six Spanish Franciscans and twenty Japanese – were crucified. "To the protests of the Governor of the Philippines," writes Sansom, "[Hideyoshi] replied that the Spaniards had no more right to introduce their religion into Japan than had the Japanese to preach the worship of their own gods in the Philippines."

127

In 1614, national unification all but complete, Hideyoshi's successor Tokugawa Ieyasu delivered the coup de grace. "The Kirishitan band," he declared, "have come to Japan... to disseminate an evil law, to overthrow true doctrine, so that they may change the government of the country... This... must be crushed."

It was. Within thirty years, Christians numbering three hundred thousand out of a total population of twenty million were either slaughtered wholesale, tortured and murdered individually, or else driven so deep underground that scarcely a trace of their existence was to surface for two hundred fifty years.

As persecution intensified, the Jesuits were nonplussed by a Japanese trait they had not previously noticed. "They race to martyrdom," observed a certain Father Organtino, "as if to a festival." The Christian view of suicide as sinful made few inroads against the traditional Japanese view of it as glorious.

"Fifty-five persons of all ages and both sexes," wrote the English trader Richard Cocks of a scene he witnessed in October 1619, "[were] burnt alive on the dry bed of the Kamo River in Kyoto, among them little children of five or six years old in their mothers' arms crying out, 'Jesus receive their souls!'"

But these public executions, the authorities soon realized, were not having their desired effect. Far from terrifying the Christians into renouncing their faith, they only made Paradise seem that much nearer. Subtler tortures were called for, and soon devised. Their aim was to induce apostasy before, or sometimes instead of, death. Three torments are especially notorious: the *onsen*, the *fumie*, and the pit.

The first amounted to being slowly boiled alive in scalding natural hot springs. The second involved having suspected Christians trample holy images of Jesus and

Mary. Refusal exposed them as Christians. Many trampled. Many refused, preferring martyrdom.

"For non-Christians," writes historian Stephen Turnbull, "stamping on the fumie eventually acquired the air of an annual ritual eagerly awaited as one of the many New Year celebrations, but to the [Christians], fumie never lost its horror, even in cases where the authorities required only the outward sign of apostasy... Prayers were said to counteract the blasphemy, and in one community there was a ritual of burning the straw sandals worn when treading on the images, mixing the ashes with water and drinking the result."

The pit was said to be the most horrible torture of all. Historian C.R. Boxer describes it: "The victim was tightly bound around the body as high as the breast (one hand being left free to give the signal of recantation) and then hung downward from a gallows into a pit which usually contained excreta and other filth, the top of the pit being level with his knees. In order to give the blood some vent, the forehead was lightly slashed with a knife. Some of the stronger martyrs lived for more than a week in this position, but the majority did not survive more than a day or two."

The "Christian Century" ends with the Shimabara rebellion of 1637-38. Ivan Morris calls it a "holocaust," a word no modern historian would use lightly. The Shimabara Peninsula in western Kyushu was then a desperately poor outback whose starved peasants were mercilessly squeezed for taxes far beyond their capacity to pay. Default invited torture as ghastly and imaginative as that meted out to Christians. How much the uprising was motivated by poverty and how much by Christian ideals remains in dispute. Its leader was a charismatic fifteen-year-old boy named Amakusa Shiro, known to his followers as "heaven's messenger." Miraculous powers were attributed to him.

Ensconced in an abandoned castle they'd seized as their stronghold were thirty-seven thousand rebels – peasants and low-ranking samurai, all at least nominally Christian. For five months they held out against impossible odds, but the end, barring a miracle, was never in doubt.

"The slaughter on 15th April [1638]," writes Morris, "was one of the greatest in all Japan's sanguinary history. The nearby rivers and inlets were clogged with decapitated bodies."

Amakusa Shiro was beheaded, his head publicly gibbeted in Nagasaki. Rebels who weren't massacred hurled themselves into the flames of the burning castle. Morris quotes a contemporary daimyo – steeped in samurai rather than Christian ideals – as commenting, "For people of their low station this was indeed a praiseworthy way of dying. Words cannot express [my admiration]."

Shimabara marks Japan's retreat into more than two hundred years of isolation from the outside world. It also marks the end, until modern times, of open Christian worship of Japan. For the next two centuries the story of Japanese Christianity is that of the *Kakure Kirishitan*, the "Hidden Christians."

(2007)

Best Friends: A Brief History of Japan-U.S. Intercourse

"How wonderful! How marvelous! From here to the southeast is what the Westerners call the Pacific Ocean and the American states! They must be very close!

– Watanabe Kazan, artist and samurai, in a diary entry recording a sojourn in Enoshima, an island off Kamakura, in 1821.

TWO MID-NINETEENTH-CENTURY WHALEMEN, an American and a Japanese, made their names immortal. Pity they never met.

They almost did. At least their paths came close to crossing.

On January 3, 1841, Herman Melville boarded the whale-ship *Acushnet* at the port of Fairhaven, Massachusetts. He was twenty-one, with not much going for him. His father had died bankrupt and the economy was still sunk under the market crash of 1837. The *Acushnet* was bound for Japan. Japan was the new horizon for American whalers, whales in the Atlantic having been hunted to near-extinction.

On January 5, 1841, a fourteen-year-old Shikoku peasant boy named Manjiro found work on an 8-meter, square-sailed fishing boat, not equipped for the deep sea because the deep sea was strictly off limits – had been ever since 1640 when *sakoku* (closed country) became the law of the land under the Tokugawa shogunate. To leave the country, or enter it, was a capital crime. But typhoons blow regardless of laws, and a particularly vicious one swept Manjiro's helpless little craft far out to sea. A desert island offered forbidding but life-saving sanctuary. Six hand-to-mouth months later, Manjiro and four companions were rescued by – coincidences are fascinatingly anarchic – another American whaler from Fairhaven, Massachusetts.

Melville never made it to Japan – he deserted the rigors of the whale ship for lushly perilous and amorous adventure among South Pacific cannibals – but Manjiro did make it to Fairhaven, taken there by his kindly rescuer, Captain William Whitfield. Whitfield found himself drawn to the young castaway with the quick intelligence and insatiable curiosity. A childless widower, he adopted the boy as a son – a gesture ironically symbolic of the bilateral relationship to come. He christened him John.

Melville, in his 1851 masterpiece *Moby Dick*, remarked, "If that double-bolted land, Japan, is ever to become hospitable, it is the whale ship alone to whom the credit will be due; for already she is on the threshold."

In 1860, an American naval officer named John Brooke noted in his journal, "I am satisfied that [John Manjiro] has had more to do with the opening of Japan than any other man living." Of the two, the latter is probably the more accurate assessment – but then Brooke was looking back, not forward. When he wrote, Japan had been "open" for six years.

"By our recent acquisitions in the Pacific, Asia has suddenly become our neighbor." – U.S. Treasury Secretary Robert Walker, 1848.

"Friend," they call each other now – the two democratic powerhouses on opposite sides of the Pacific. *Tomodachi* means "friend" in Japanese, and in giving that name to the vast relief operation its military launched following the March 11, 2011 earthquake and tsunami, the United States seemed to be saying, "We're more than just allies."

That's part spin, part plain truth. There really is a special relationship between these two nations. There is one, too, between the U.S. and Britain – based on common language, culture, values. What is the Japan-U.S. relationship based on?

Opposites. Can any two nations be more diametrically opposed? That's less true today, Japan in defeat having adopted many of the victor's ways. Clashing contraries remain all the same, as the trade friction of the 1980s and the seemingly intractable tensions over American military bases show. But they clash less harshly. If the two nations bewilder, annoy and irritate each other now, imagine the confusion attending their first acquaintance.

Whatever one was, the other was not, and vice versa. America was new, Japan old: America expansive, Japan insular; America rich, Japan poor: America big, Japan small; America individualist, Japan collective: America multi-ethnic, Japan proudly mono-cultural. America's highest ideal was freedom, Japan's obedience; the U.S. gloried in the pursuit of happiness, Japan in self-sacrifice – and so on and so on. Japan was "the land of the gods," America a "city on a hill." They seemed destined to despise each other, and sometimes did, but more often didn't. That's the wonder of Japan-U.S. relations.

They began with a rape dressed up as seduction – and accepted as such, over time. The story is familiar. Four words and it's told: Commodore Perry, Black Ships. That leaves blanks to fill in, of course, among them the inexhaustible energy of young America, scarcely comprehensible in the present old age of mankind. A new nation was bursting its seams; a huge continent was too small for it. By 1848 California was American, following a victorious war with Mexico. What next? The Pacific. To Americans of that day, the Far East was the Far West. The letter that Commodore Matthew Perry brought from U.S. President Millard Fillmore for the Emperor of Japan in July 1853 declared – not in so many words but in effect: We're on our way, cooperate or else: you're either for us or against us.

"You know," Fillmore wrote to the Emperor Komei – who, unknown to the Americans, sat impotent in Kyoto; power resided with the shogun in Edo (soon to become Tokyo), who, unknown to himself, was rapidly losing control of events – "that the United States of America now extend from sea to sea; that the great countries of Oregon & California are parts of the United States; and that from these countries, which are rich in gold & silver & precious stones, our steamers can reach the shores of your happy land in less than 20 days…"

Engaged mainly in trade with China, these steamers, the president continued, "must pass along the Coast of your Empire; storms & winds may cause them to be wrecked on your shores, and we ask & expect from your kindness & your greatness, kindness for our men…

"Your Empire has a great abundance of coal; this is an article which our Steamships in going from California to China, must use…"

How many Japanese at the time could even imagine what steamships were? In 1851, the year *Moby Dick* was published, John Manjiro, having acquired an American education, having gone a-whaling, having made a modest fortune in the 1849 California gold rush, returned to Japan – on a whale-ship, as it happened, so Melville may have been right after all. He landed under cover of night on a beach in Okinawa, made his way to Kagoshima in the south of Kyushu, and was interrogated by the local ruler, Lord Shimazu, to whom the wonder of steam power came as an astonishing revelation. Yes, said Manjiro, the Americans had ocean-going steamships; also "land ships," which ran on iron rails.

"Comrade Americanos – to us, then, at last, the Orient comes…" – American poet Walt Whitman, 1860.

Perry and his men laid out Japan's first "iron rails" on the beach at Yokohama. It was March, 1854, barely nine months after Perry had delivered his letter and promised – threatened, rather – to return the following year. Now the "Black Ships" were back.

An exchange of gifts and entertainments was preliminary to the signing of the Treaty of Peace and Amity wrested at last from a grudging, stalling but helpless Japan. Manjiro, newly dubbed a samurai, served as the shogun's interpreter – despite reservations in some quarters. "I wonder," mused one official, "if that American barbarian" – Manjiro's foster-father, Whitfield – "educated Manjiro as part of some scheme."

The miniature locomotive the Americans set running on those iron rails was a hit. "It was a spectacle not a little ludicrous," noted the official *Narrative of the*

Expedition, "to behold a dignified mandarin whirling around the circular road at the rate of twenty miles an hour, with his loose robes flying in the wind."

The Japanese were all admiration, the Americans all contempt. A staged sumo contest, meant to impress, fell flat. "From the brutal performance of the wrestlers," says the *Narrative*, "the Americans turned with pride to the exhibition... of the telegraph and the railroad. It was a happy contrast, which a higher civilization presented, to the disgusting display on the part of the Japanese officials. In place of a show of brute animal force, there was a triumphant revelation, to a partially enlightened people, of the success of science and enterprise."

The two nations stood face to face and yet did not see each other. Is it surprising? To each the other represented barbarism.

A trivial but revealing example: The Japanese "are a *clean* people," wrote U.S. Consul Townsend Harris, recording his first impressions upon arrival in 1856 to negotiate a trade treaty supplementary to the Peace and Amity pact. "Everyone bathes every day... [People] of both sexes, old and young, enter the same bathroom and there perform their ablution in a state of perfect nudity. I cannot account for so indelicate a proceeding on the part of a people so generally correct."

Four years later, a Japanese delegation, seventy-seven strong, Manjiro among them as chief interpreter, traveled to the U.S. to formally ratify the treaty Harris had finally succeeded in imposing. (The stalling tactics with which his Japanese interlocutors tortured him were beyond anything they had dared risk with Perry – who, unlike Harris, had been authorized to use force if necessary. One can hardly blame the Japanese; they were doing what little they could, including trying to soften Harris with a geisha mistress, to protect themselves against such treaty provisions as

American-controlled tariffs and the surrender of jurisdiction over criminal proceedings involving foreigners.)

> *Over the Western sea hither from Niphon come,*
> *Courteous, the swart-cheek'd two-sworded envoys"*

sang Whitman, poetically celebrating the delegation's arrival in New York. Whose proceedings are "indelicate"? One Japanese delegate was shocked to observe, during a dance, that American women "were nude from shoulders to arms… The way men and women, both young and old, mixed in the dance was simply insufferable to watch."

"For the next generation the Japanese we knew will be as extinct as Belemnites." – Dr. William Sturgis Bigelow in a letter to Edward Sylvester Morse, circa 1883.

We move on now to a cast of characters whose most familiar representative is Lafcadio Hearn – the American (or American-based) Japanophiles of the late nineteenth and early twentieth centuries. Gone is the facile contempt that marked the initial encounters; in its stead, an intense appreciation, germinating in New England and spreading outward, of Japanese art, Japanese thought, the mysterious way the Japanese had of making so little express so much, the mysterious Japanese *beauty*. America in comparison – the nouveau-riche, hyperactive, proto-industrial America of the post-Civil War "Gilded Age" – seemed, to some sensitive souls at least, uncouth, empty, ugly.

This is a long way to have come in thirty years from the smug superiority of the days of the Black Ships. Which was the "higher civilization" after all?

The irony is that most Japanese were by this time thinking like the *Narrative of the Expedition.* Japanese contempt for Japanese culture had become poisonous. Japanese art in Japanese eyes was "backward," "feudal," fussy, trifling, an obstacle to progress. American collectors were buying Japanese pictures, statues, porcelains for a song; the Japanese couldn't unload their treasures fast enough.

"Belemnites" are a species of extinct mollusks. Edward Sylvester Morse was a biologist, an early Darwinian. Dr. William Sturgis Bigelow, one of his many disciples in Japanophilia, was a surgeon. "I first visited Japan solely for the purpose of studying various species of Brachiopods in the Japan Seas," Morse wrote. It was in 1877, a year after the Philadelphia World's Fair. "The Japanese exhibit at the Centennial exposition in Philadelphia," he recalled, "came to us as a revelation."

Lafcadio Hearn had a similar awakening at another World's Fair – New Orleans, 1884. The electric lights on dazzling display there gave him nightmares. "Never," he wrote, "did the might of machinery seem to me so awful as when I first watched that enormous incandescence." The Japanese exhibit soothed him. He and his soon-to-be-adopted country shared an affinity for shadows – waxing in his case, waning in Japan's, though he refused to acknowledge it. Japan, he wrote years later, willfully blind to brute fact, "remains just as Oriental today as she was a thousand years ago."

And so 1877 found Morse in Japan. Tokyo Imperial University, ancestor of today's University of Tokyo, was then all of three years old. It had hired him to lecture on Darwinism. The character of this remarkable man, well described by the American scholar Christopher Benfy in

The Great Wave (2003), is an inspiration to all cross-cultural wanderers. His refusal – more an innate inability – to view Japan through the filter of presumed Western and Christian superiority made him the father of American Japanophilia. His profession did not define him. Everything in the world interested him. He was the first foreigner to study Noh drama, the first foreigner to study tea ceremony. "The Japanese," he observed, "enjoy the natural results of nature's caprices." They seemed to him instinctive Darwinists. He admired Japanese pottery and became an avid collector. He wrote a book titled *Japanese Homes and their Surroundings* (1885) that celebrated – perhaps for the first time outside Japan – sparsity.

"Our American rooms," he wrote, "seem to [the Japanese] like a curiosity shop. Such a maze of vases, pictures, plaques, bronzes, with shelves, brackets, cabinets and tables loaded down with bric-a-brac, is quite enough to drive a Japanese frantic."

The list of American artists, architects and collectors whose appreciation of Japan began with or was enriched by Morse is long and distinguished. It includes the art critic and scholar Ernest Fenellosa, artist John LaFarge, art collector Isabella Gardner, architect Frank Lloyd Wright. Thanks to them, says Benfy, the Museum of Fine Arts in Boston houses "the greatest and most comprehensive repository of Japanese art outside Japan." Furthermore, "All across New England.. one finds vestiges of Japanese practices in rooflines and sheds, balconies and alcoves, and in a willingness to leave empty space for the imagination to dwell in."

Empty space is an acquired taste. Americans aren't bred on it, and some, probably most, see nothing in it. One, writing in an expatriate Yokohama newspaper in 1881, observed, "The Japanese are a happy race, and being content with little, are unlikely to achieve much."

"Th' trouble is whin the gallant Commodore [Perry] kicked opn th' door, we didn't go in. They came out." – Finley Peter Dunne, Irish-American humorist, 1907.

Come out they did. They burst their bonds. Bullied into "civilization," the Japanese soared to the challenge and became bullies in turn, defeating China in 1895, Russia ten years later. "A subjick race is on'y funny whin it's raaly subjeck," observed Dunne's fictional alter ego, Chicago saloon-keeper Mr. Dooley. "About three years ago [1904] I stopped laughin' at Japanese jokes."

Cheering Japan on – at first – was U.S. President Theodore Roosevelt. "Banzai!" he wrote to his Japanophile friend Bigelow in 1905 as Japan bore down on the Russians. Bigelow, playing on Roosevelt's admiration for virility in all its manifestations, had introduced the warrior president (fresh from victory over Spain in 1898) to Japanese warrior culture, his intention being to influence American foreign policy in Japan's favor. He succeeded – thus unwittingly contributing to the very "extinction" he had foreseen with dread twenty years earlier.

When Japan in 1904 struck a Russian-leased port in Korea without so much as a declaration of war, the U.S. was quietly approving – on the grounds, said the American minister in Japan, that "these people [Koreans] cannot govern themselves."

Victory in war conferred worthiness to govern others. This was a species of Darwinism – political survival of the fittest – that Morse had not taught at Tokyo Imperial University. Victorious Japan had proved, in the words of one Japanese official, that "civilization is not a monopoly of the white man."

In 1906 came a crisis. Japanese emigrants had been settling in California since the 1880s, and by 1900 numbered about twenty-four thousand. There was resentment. Japanese "labor for less than a white man can live on," said the San Francisco Chronicle, prime stoker of fears of the "Yellow Peril." In April 1906 an earthquake leveled San Francisco; six months later the local Board of Education, on the pretext of damage to schools, "ordered that all Chinese, Japanese and Korean children go (sometimes at great distance) to a segregated Oriental Public School," writes American historian Walter Lafeber in *The Clash: U.S.-Japanese Relations Throughout History* (1997). "The timing was not thoughtful: Japan's Red Cross had just sent a quarter-million dollars" to aid quake victims. "The Japanese government strongly protested the segregation of its citizens. A leading Tokyo newspaper cried: 'Stand up, Japanese nation! Our countrymen have been *humiliated!*'"

Roosevelt raged at the "idiots" in California – but he took note of Japanese ire and prepared for war. Cooler thinking prevailed, resulting in a "Gentlemen's Agreement" (as it was termed) which saw the segregation order withdrawn in exchange for a Japanese commitment to voluntarily restrict emigration.

But racism is a powerful force. Presidential candidate Woodrow Wilson, campaigning in California in 1912, said, "Oriental coolieism will give us another race problem to solve, and surely we have had our lesson." In 1913 the state legislature passed a bill prohibiting land purchases by Japanese. (The fact that foreigners were prohibited from owning land in Japan did not, apparently, mitigate Japanese anger.) In 1924 the U.S. Immigration Act banned Japanese immigration nationwide, until it was at last withdrawn in 1952.

It was a blow. Yusuke Tsurumi, critic, writer and future politician, made no secret of that in lectures across the U.S. immediately after the Act's passage. "To my Oriental mind," he said, "the procedure of Congress is inexplicable... By a curious coincidence, the Immigration Act broke in upon the meditations of the Japanese people at a moment when the nation was bleeding from the wounds inflicted by the greatest calamity ever visited upon mankind by earthquake and fire" – the Great Kanto Earthquake of September 1923.

"In the midst of our afflictions, the nation that had literally shaken open our gate, introduced us to the family of nations, sent Christian missionaries to teach us the ways of brotherhood and peace, and given us friendly counsel and advice at every turn... slammed its own gate shut in our face."

"In the first six to twelve months of a war with the United States and Britain, I will run wild and win victory after victory. But if the war continues after that, I have no expectation of success." – Admiral Isoruku Yamamoto, September 1940, warning Prime Minister Fumimaro Konoe that a war with the West was unwinnable.

His warning overruled, Yamamoto became the reluctant mastermind of the surprise attack on Pearl Harbor, Hawaii.

"Yesterday, December 7, 1941 – a date which will live in infamy – the United States of America was suddenly and deliberately attacked by... the Empire of Japan." – U.S. President Franklin D. Roosevelt to Congress, reacting to Pearl Harbor.

"This war will give us much trouble in the future. The fact that we have had a small success at Pearl Harbor is nothing." – Admiral Yamamoto.

"If only we might fall like cherry blossoms in spring – so pure and radiant!" – haiku by a kamikaze pilot who died in combat in February 1945, age 22.

"This year when they turn on the lights of the Christmas tree in Rockefeller Center, we Americans are going to have to come to grips with the reality that this great national celebration is actually occurring on Japanese property." – Connecticut Senator Joseph Lieberman, 1989.

There is nothing in history quite like Japan-U.S. relations. Sometimes it seems less like a relationship between nations than one between two people, characterized by convoluted human psychology rather than cold realpolitik. They have felt for each other, at different times and sometimes simultaneously, admiration and contempt, affection and repugnance, fascination and bewilderment, trust and distrust. Each has learned from the other, been appalled by the other, and striven to imitate the other.

When force was involved, it was generally America that applied it and Japan that either yielded or was crushed. In terms of influence, there seems little doubt that Japan is more Americanized than America is Japanized (America's ubiquitous sushi bars notwithstanding). And yet the rabid popularity in America of manga and anime reminds us of an earlier

143

wave of American appreciation of Japanese art, and suggests something enduring.

Even in the field of industrial capitalism – which Japan, naturally given to the sparsity and restraint so admired by Morse and Hearn, had to learn from scratch from American masters operating in their native element of limitless production and insatiable consumption – *Japan As Number One* was not only the title of a 1979 bestselling book by Harvard sociologist Ezra Vogel but a slogan that expressed a development that looked increasingly likely as the 1980s advanced. Then Japan slipped and the likelihood receded, but it had been real enough. "Please, Japan. Return the favor. Occupy us," editorialized the New York Times in March 1981.

The U.S. Occupation of Japan from 1945 to 1952 was, in the words of British historian Richard Storry, "the most harmonious occupation of one great country by another that has ever been known." It and the subsequent course of the relationship, given the bottomless hatred and wholesale destruction that had preceded it, "almost seems a small miracle," wrote American historian John Dower. Why "almost," and why "small"? This is as miraculous as international relations get. From Pearl Harbor and Hiroshima-Nagasaki to the quasi-adoption that followed the war – the U.S. playing Captain Whitfield to Japan's Manjiro – is an extraordinary leap, and the two nations that made it made history in so doing.

The sailing hasn't been smooth. Communist China "red or green" was "a natural market," defiantly declared Japan's first postwar prime minister, Shigeru Yoshida, in 1949 – "and it has become necessary for Japan to think about markets."

That stunned the Americans. Was Japan forgetting itself? Was evil – in communist guise – to be accommodated rather than uprooted?

144

The first thirty years of bilateral postwar diplomacy can be summed up in terms of American efforts to keep Japan on its side of the Cold War. The carrot was trade concessions. The stick included U.S. threats, as when Japan refused to send troops to the Vietnam War, to pull out of Asia altogether and leave Japan to face an expansionist China alone.

Yet while American markets opened to Japanese goods, Japanese markets remained stubbornly closed, Japanese negotiators tying their American interlocutors up in knots with the same faultlessly polite immovability that had so frustrated Perry and Harris more than a hundred years before – only now the Japanese had cards to play and the Americans huffed and puffed in vain.

The concessions won set the stage for the trade friction of the second thirty years of bilateral postwar diplomacy. Japan was getting a free ride, Americans fumed as their economy sputtered and Japan's soared. U.S. President Richard Nixon in 1971 gave Japan all of three minutes' advance notice before announcing U.S. recognition of China – his way, he said, to "stick it to Japan" for Japan's failure to voluntarily reduce textile exports flooding American markets. Japanese cars ruled American roads – another sore point. "When you bought your Japanese car, ten Americans lost their jobs," read a 1980s American bumper sticker. Japanese capital seemed to be buying up America – the Rockefeller Center was the last straw for Senator Joseph Lieberman. What was this, Pearl Harbor all over again? "The Japanese are still fighting the war, only now instead of a shooting war it is an economic war," said Maurice Stans, Nixon's Commerce Secretary, in 1971.

Where would it have ended, had Japan's economy in the 1990s not sickened and foundered? There is no telling. Perhaps friendship of this kind depends on one

party being weak and dependent and knowing its place –
in which case the other party will be all benevolence.

(2011)

Refuge

THE MAIN CHARACTER of the one-act play that follows is loosely based on the few known facts concerning a Russian nobleman-refugee named Semyon Nikolaevitch Smirnitsky. Born in St. Petersburg in 1879, Smirnitsky fled the Russian Revolution in 1919 and spent the rest of his life in Japan, mostly in Otaru, Hokkaido, as a teacher of Russian at Otaru Commercial High School, today's Otaru Commercial College. His personality was at least remarkable enough to have inspired some of his students to write affectionate, if patchy, memoirs about him. After World War Two he was briefly detained on an apparently baseless suspicion of spying for the Soviet Union. He died in 1948.

All characters other than "Smir-*sensei*" are entirely fictitious.

Scene 1:
Late afternoon of a day in early February 1932, dusk just beginning to fall. Ono, muffled and hunched against the cold, walks rapidly along a narrow street, frozen snow crunching underfoot. As he approaches his destination his pace slows and he seems to hesitate. He turns into the walkway of a large two-story wooden Japanese-style house. At the door he hesitates again, then pulls the bell handle. No answer. He rings again. Still no answer. Gingerly

he tries the door, which slides open. He steps inside. Suddenly a monkey springs at him; Ono screams, but at once recovers himself.

Ono: Oh, it's you, Tolstoy. Where's Smir-sensei? *(looks at his watch)* It's five o'clock. *(turning to two boys, Takahashi and Yano, approaching from behind)* Sensei's not here.

Takahashi: Let's go inside, I'm freezing.

Ono: We can't just walk in...

Takahashi: Sure we can! "Make yourselves at home," he's always saying. Isn't he?

Yano: "My home is your home." *(He brushes past Ono and leads the way through a long corridor into a very large kitchen. Little animals scurry about everywhere — rabbits, small dogs, cats. The wood-burning stove is glowing; it's very hot. The boys remove their coats; they are wearing high school uniforms. On the large table are strewn pots and pans and cooking utensils of all kinds, as though the occupant of the house had been in the midst of preparing a meal. The monkey chatters volubly.)*

Yano: Sh, quiet, Tolstoy!

Ono: He fixed the time himself, didn't he? Can't he at least...

Takahashi: Where's Pushkin?

Yano: *(snickering)* Taking a nap in the study, maybe.

Ono: *(kicking aside a clinging dog)* Is this a house or a zoo? Who's that? *(enter Inoue)*

Inoue: Tagawa will be along in a minute. He stopped at the pharmacist's to get his medicine. Where's Smir-sensei?

Takahashi: Ask Tolstoy here.

Yano: He knows, but doesn't speak our language.

Takahashi: Let's go into the study and see the snakes.

Ono: *(irritated)* Never mind the snakes. We're here to –

Yano: Here's Tagawa. Did you get your epilepsy medicine? You're not going to have a fit or anything, are you?

Tagawa: *(mildly)* I don't have epilepsy, I have asthma. I don't have fits.

Ono: We're here to rehearse. The play is in three weeks; we haven't even started re –

Takahashi: How can we rehearse? We don't have a script.

Ono: We should have had a script weeks ago!

Yano: The trouble with you, Ono, is you're too serious. If Smir-sensei has anything to teach us, besides Russian, it's that life is a comedy! Being serious is not – *(The sudden noise of someone furiously flinging open a door. Enter a man in a Russian fur hat and long overcoat. Tall, imposing and heavily bearded, he speaks Japanese with a heavy Russian accent.)*

Man: *(glaring fiercely)* Arrest them! You are friends of Smirnitsky? Eh? Well? Smirnitsky has been arrested! He has confessed! He is a spy! You are all spies – traitors! To the firing squad with them! The firing squad! *(He roars with laughter, removes his hat, rips of his false beard)* Ha ha! *(speaking now with scarcely a trace of an accent)* Ha ha! You'd think you'd be wise to my little pranks by now. *(removes his coat, tosses it carelessly over the back of a chair)* Tolstoy! Ah, you are glad to see me! How is Pushkin doing? *(to the boys)* Pushkin is not well. I am worried about him. He is dull, listless, not himself... Let's go into the study and see how – Pushkin! *(enter a second monkey, yawning and rubbing his eyes)* You've had a nap, you look better! Doesn't he look better, Tolstoy? Yes, yes, yes... *(to the boys)* Just before, he seemed so out of sorts that I ran to consult my friend Dr. Kondo. That is why I am late. Kondo will come and look at him later this evening... *(to Pushkin, stroking the monkey's head)* But now I look at you and wonder if there is any need to trouble him. What do you think, boy, eh?

Ono: Sensei...

Smir: Yes, Ono-kun.

Ono: Sensei, forgive me, but... *(embarrassed)* the play is in three weeks...

Smir: Plenty of time, plenty of time!

Ono: But we are not actors, like you.

Smir: Like me! Ha ha ha!

Ono: *(doggedly, eyes lowered)* And we are not Russian-speakers. We need time to prepare, learn our lines, rehearse.

Smir: Quite right. I ask your pardon. Come into the study. You will see I have not been idle. Begging forgiveness of the divine Chekhov as I worked, I have prepared an abridged, simplified version of his immortal play *Uncle Vanya*. There are copies for everyone. Two nights in a row I was up, writing copies – and yet I don't feel tired, not in the least! It was as if Chekhov himself was in the room with me. You have of course all read the play in Japanese – yes? Takahashi-kun! I have a special favor to ask you. You mustn't refuse me. I want you to take the part of Sonya. *(muted snickering)*

Takahashi: Me?

Smir: You!

Takahashi: Play a woman?

Smir: Trust my instincts, Takahashi-kun! And my makeup skills too, which... well, you will see. You will see! A sudden inspiration I had: this part is for Takahashi, Takahashi and no one else, because Takahashi is sensitive and... She is a plain woman, you see, in love with a man, *passionately* in love with a man, who does not love her. Ah, if only she were good-looking, if only she were beautiful! It is tragic. You must play her with delicacy, subtlety, *nuance*...

Takahashi: But... sensei...

Smir: "But sensei, I am not a woman!" Of course you are not a woman! You are Takahashi. Does that mean that on stage you can be only Takahashi? Is that

150

theater – Takahashi being Takahashi? In the theater we leave reality behind, we create new reality! That is what… *(the doorbell rings)* Ah! That will be Dr. Kondo. Excuse me. *(exit)*

Yano: *(mockingly)* Delicacy! Subtlety! Nuance!

Takahashi: *(grumbling)* I'm not playing Sonya.

Yano: Theater, Takahashi, theater! Leave reality behind! Theater! Ha ha! *(Enter Smirnitsky and Kondo, conversing, to the boys' surprise, in Russian.)*

Smir: Boys, this is Dr. Kondo. I have known him many years, his wife is Russian, he is the best veterinarian in all Otaru, if not all Japan. Pushkin! Come, we will go into the study and have Dr. Kondo examine you – though really, Kondo-san, I am afraid I have troubled you for nothing. Excuse me, boys, for just a few minutes. Start reading among yourselves. I will be with you presently. *(exit)*

Tagawa: I want to play Professor Serebryakov. He's old and ill…

Yano: And you're young and ill.

Inoue: That'd make you Takahashi's papa. *(re-enter Smirnitsky, flurried, with papers)*

Smir: Here, I forgot… *(distributes papers)* Start reading, start reading! *(exits hurriedly)*

Takahashi: I'm not playing Sonya. Let Ono play her. He has the face of a girl.

Yano: He has delicacy, but he lacks subtlety and nuance. Whereas you…

Ono: Shut up, Yano!

Yano: Oh dear, oh dear! Ono-kun is angry! Help! He is going to strike me with his handkerchief! *(Ono abruptly snatches his coat and makes as if to leave)*

Inoue: Wait! *(holds him by the arm)* Come, Ono's right. Enough fooling. Let's get down to work. Takahashi, you're being stupid. Since there are only boys enrolled in

151

Smir-sensei's Russian course, we might have expected that some of us would have to play women.

Tagawa: Didn't he say that some of his Russian friends would join us? I thought...

Inoue: I'd be happy to play a woman. It'll be fun. I'll volunteer for Marina, the old servant. Don't kabuki actors play women? It's a role, a performance, it's nothing to... Ono, what... you're crying!

Ono: *(sobbing openly, wrenching his arm from Inoue's grasp)* Leave me alone! Do you think I enrolled in this course to... to... Do you think I... *(sniffs, wipes his eyes, masters his emotion: quietly)* I will tell you why I enrolled in this course. I am a Communist! A Marxist! I believe in the regeneration of mankind through *socialism*, and I long passionately to emigrate to the Soviet Union. *(The others gaze at him in utter stupefaction. Ono resumes, after a short silence, defiantly)* Go ahead, denounce me to the police, have me arrested! You all think I'm weak, but even if they torture me to death I will never renounce my beliefs. *(silence)* I hope they *do* torture me! *(silence)*

Tagawa: *(incredulously)* You want to emigrate to the Soviet Union?

Takahashi: To live under Stalin?

Inoue: After what Sensei said?

Takahashi: Starvation, mass killings...

Ono: *(grumbling)* Don't believe everything Sensei says.

Tagawa: He ought to know, he..."

Ono: *(flaring up)* Sensei is an aristocrat, an enemy of the people! For hundreds of years he and his kind fattened off the toil of the working class. Now at last...

Tagawa: Sensei, an enemy of the people?

Yano: Sensei fat?

Takahashi: Is this Ono speaking? Or is it some imposter pretending to be Ono?

Inoue: It sure isn't the Ono we know.

Ono: The Ono you *think* you know. No, it isn't! In secret I have read, studied, thought. And you? You see only the surface, which means you see nothing. Nothing! Nothing! You do not understand the revolution's great goal, which is… which is… to regenerate mankind! To regenerate the soul! Laugh, go ahead! To root out egoism and selfishness and build in its place a… a collective soul, a collective personality! A collective personality that – *(A door is heard opening.)* Sh! *(Smirnitsky enters, looking grim, followed by Kondo.)*

Smir: Boys, my deepest, deepest apologies. I have received news, I must leave you. We will resume our rehearsal… today is Sunday… Wednesday, after class. Truly, I am sorry. If there was any way… But there is time. There is still, fortunately, plenty of time. Trust me.

Inoue: Is it Pushkin?

Smir: *(brightening slightly)* Oh no! No, Pushkin is quite well, thanks be to God! Pushkin will be fine. Dr. Kondo! *(he shakes the doctor's hand, vigorously)* I thank you again and again, for everything. For everything, do you hear?

Kondo: I will see you, then, at Otaru Station, at eight o'clock sharp.

Smir: *(seeing him out)* Yes, yes, eight o'clock sharp.

Takahashi; Sensei?

Smir: Yes, Takahashi-kun.

Takahashi: Sensei, I have thought it over. I was being childish. I beg your pardon. I will play Sonya if you want me to, if you think…

Smir: *(brightening still more)* Excellent! I am so pleased. But for now, *(somberly)* I am afraid I must say goodbye. I was so hoping to begin rehearsals today, and then *(indicating the clutter on the table)* to cook you all a genuine Russian dinner. Well, Wednesday after class! We have plenty of time. Inoue, I have you in mind for the part of Dr. Astrov. Think it over. Goodbye, goodbye. Tagawa,

153

give my regards to your father… Ono-kun, would you remain behind for just a few minutes? I would like a word with you. Come into the study.

Scene 2:

The study is almost as large as the kitchen, but so heavily furnished, so cluttered, as to seem confining. It is conspicuously un-Japanese. A heavy curtain along one wall gives a sense of total, almost cavelike enclosure.

The floor is covered by a thick Persian carpet. A stove blazes; like the kitchen, it is somewhat overheated and stuffy. In the center of the room is a remarkably large wooden desk, strewn with papers and books. Along two of the walls are bookcases stuffed and overflowing with books. Along another is a thick leather sofa. On top of the bookcases and here and there on the floor are fish tanks and other receptacles for holding snakes, turtles, lizards… Hanging on one wall is a reproduction of Perov's famous portrait of Dostoevsky. Long-bearded, wrapped in an overcoat, the writer sits with one leg folded over the other, his hands clasped on his knee – the very picture of tense self-consciousness.

Beside the portrait is a large, old-fashioned grandfather clock, which ticks loudly in the silence of the room. The dim lighting comes from a floor lamp behind the desk.

Smirnitsky and Ono are seated opposite each other on two heavy armchairs. Unconsciously, Ono sit in much the same posture as Dostoevsky, and looks no less ill at ease; the contrast this poses between youth and age is touching and a little comical. Pushkin, still a little under the weather, reclines on the sofa. Tolstoy, restless, chatters and makes a nuisance of himself, Smirnitsky hardly seeming not to notice. Rabbits, cats and dogs come and go unregarded.

Smir: Am I keeping you from anything, Ono-kun?

Ono: *(looking about as though for a means of escape)* No... well, actually...

Smir: Sit with me for a few minutes. I won't keep you long. *(pause)* I feel somehow drawn to you... You remind me of my son... You don't know, Ono, and I hope you never learn, how – what is the word I am looking for? Lonely, of course, but... something more. The loneliness of exile... I hope you never know it – it is like no other loneliness. But these times are like no other times. One cannot be sure of anything.

Ono: Your son?

Smir: You are surprised. I have never spoken of my family. I have three children – two boys and a girl. Yes.

Ono: Where are they?

Smir: In Russia. St. Petersburg – Leningrad, they call it now. It is my younger son you remind me of. He is just about your age. Tolstoy, be quiet! My wife, when I fled Russia in 1919, refused to leave. She was a true revolutionary, a true believer. Had the occasion arisen, she would without hesitation have informed on me as a counter-revolutionary – without hesitation; and it's not that she did not love me! Oh no, she did. I daresay she loves me still. And would inform on me still. *(dreamily)* Tell me, Ono-kun: do you believe in God?

Ono: *(confused)* In God? The Christian God?

Smir: In God. Not this God or that God, your God or my God... God. I myself did not believe, Ono, and I mocked the fools who did. But here is what I know now: man without God is monstrous. Man *must* believe in God. It's not a question of, does the idea appeal to you, does it make sense logically, is it consistent with the precepts of science. We *must* believe. Because without God... *Lenin* becomes God, *Stalin* becomes God. Yes, strange as it may seem, it is Lenin and Stalin who made me believe in God. *(strained silence)* You are wondering why I am telling you this, why I single you out from the others to tell you this. Are you not? Well, first of all, as I said, you remind me, for some mysterious reason, of my son. So there is something in me that yearns to tell you all the things I would tell him, all the things I have learned about life…

But there is something else. *(pause)* Something else… I myself hardly know what. It is as if…I seem to see you as though in a dream. I see you on the edge of a precipice, and I have an impulse to reach out a hand to you, to steady you, to pull you back… Speak to me, Ono-kun. You know how fond I am of you.

Ono: *(agitated)* I… I too… I mean…

Smir: Your heart is troubled. Is it not?

Ono: I… *(breaks off)*

Smir: *(after a pause)* I must go to Hakodate tonight. Dr. Kondo has asked me to accompany him. Some men, Russians, came ashore in a fishing boat. They seek asylum. Alas, Japan no longer grants asylum to Russians fleeing Stalin's earthly paradise. Tokyo officially recognized the Soviet Union in 1925. The men will no doubt be forcibly repatriated. That is what is done nowadays. It is a death sentence – they will be shot as soon as they arrive. Or sent to a labor camp, which is worse.

The Hokkaido Russian Immigrant Society, in which Dr. Kondo and his wife are very active, and I too, in a small way… the Society has offered to raise money to ship the prisoners to Shanghai, or some other neutral port. The Japanese have refused. They say it would harm relations with the Soviet Union. Dr. Kondo thinks perhaps I can persuade them.

It is useless, hopeless. Who am I? What can I say? Still, I must do what I can. *(pause)* Ono… what happened in Russia in 1917, 1918, 1919 – what is happening there still – the chaos, the madness, the… the evil… it is not possible to describe such things to someone who has known only settled times. Engulfed by chaos, engulfed by

156

evil, I failed – failed my own children. I failed them. Yes. I would like, if possible, not to fail you. *(pause)* Won't you tell me? Shall I guess, then? You have been seduced by the illusion of the earthly paradise, you have been seduced by Stalin: he is your god, your sun...

Ono: *(passionately)* Yes! Yes! I will go to the Soviet Union and help build the earthly paradise that you – like all aristocrats who despise the people – revile! It is my dream! Long live Stalin! And death to... to...

Smir: *(calmly)* To his enemies? To me? *(He rises to his feet, goes to his desk, and from a drawer withdraws a revolver, which he hands to Ono.)* Take it. It is loaded. I am a Russian officer who knows how to face death, and I trust in God to send it at the right time. *(resumes his seat; pause)* That is not how you aim a gun. Here, let me show you. Good heavens! You're trembling, you're pale... Well, here, give it back to me then. Let us put it back where it came from *(he does so)* and forget that it exists.

Your heart is good, Ono. I knew that it was. Had I doubted it, I would not have thrown away my life so lightly. I love life, you see, though it mocks my love and sends me sorrow upon sorrow. We will talk further of this another time. Come, Ono, you mustn't... *(Ono is sobbing helplessly)* Come. It is getting late. I must prepare food for my menagerie. I will return Tuesday evening. On Wednesday we will begin rehearsing in earnest. You will see. All will go well. We have plenty of time.

(2009)

Ero-Guro & Other Nonsense: Taisho Japan

"Democracy is so popular these days!"
— The Democracy Song, 1919

ON JULY 30, 1912 Emperor Meiji passed away and Japan, traveling blind, entered a new age. The Taisho Era (1912-26), sandwiched between the boldly modernizing Meiji Era (1868-1912) and the militarist tide of early Showa (the Showa Era ran from1926 to 1989), deserves more recognition than it gets.

Taisho is Japan's Jazz Age. Can it be summed up in a phrase? It often is: *ero-guro-nansensu* — eroticism, grotesquerie, nonsense.

All three filled the air. Was Taisho, then, mere frivolity? To cite only the plainest evidence to the contrary: World War One; the 1918 Rice Riots; "Taisho Democracy"; the founding in 1922 of the Japan Communist Party; the Great Kanto Earthquake of 1923; the granting of universal manhood suffrage in 1925; and the repressive Peace Preservation Law passed barely two months later.

Taisho's turbulence was of an intensity and significance way out of proportion to its brevity. It was a revolution — a failed revolution, as the militarism of the 1930s was to show. Meanwhile, exuberance reigned — exuberance of a peculiar kind. Something of its spirit comes across in the reaction of novelist Junichiro

Tanizaki (1886-1965) to the earthquake which incinerated much of his native Tokyo, killing roughly a hundred thousand people: "Almost simultaneously I felt a deep surge of happiness which I could not keep down. 'Tokyo will be the better for this!' I said to myself."

A child as Taisho dawned would have had grandparents molded by the Edo Period (1603-1867), living symbols of how startlingly Japan had changed within living memory. Edo Japan, closed to the outside world and drifting in a samurai and Confucian time warp, would have seemed almost as archaic to Emperor Taisho's subjects as it does to us. In 1912 only fifty-eight years had passed since the United States pried Japan open like a rusty sardine can. Between Edo and Taisho stood the stern and patriarchal Meiji Era, surely one of the most energetic regimes in world history. Historian Richard Storry, in *A History of Modern Japan* (1960), enumerates the most visible innovations – many others, institutional and psychological, were less visible – of Meiji's first two decades: "Banks, railways, harbors, lighthouses, dockyards, telegraph offices, printing presses and newspapers, post offices, cigars and cigarettes – the entire apparatus of Western material civilization seemed to find some reproduction, some kind of echo, in Japan."

Such was Meiji. The emperor posthumously named for the era (he was Emperor Mutsuhito while he lived) was a grave, dignified figure. Actual power was wielded not by him and certainly not by "the people." It was wielded by a narrowly exclusive oligarchy – but Emperor Meiji was a worthy symbol of the modernization effected in his name, and of the era's most characteristic slogan: "Rich country, strong army."

160

His son and successor, Emperor Yoshihito (posthumously Taisho), marked a shift of gears – or maybe the stripping of gears. A bout of cerebral meningitis as an infant left him with lifelong brain damage. Lucid intervals alternated with spells when no one quite knew what he would do. A characteristic story is of him attending a Diet session and peering at the proceedings through a rolled-up document, as through a telescope. He was unpresentable, and more or less faded from public view, a skeleton in the nation's closet. (From 1921 until his death on Christmas Day 1926 his son, the future Emperor Showa, served as regent.) If a "Jazz Age" is to bloom under a divine emperor, it probably should be one like Emperor Taisho.

Ero-guro-nansensu – where to begin? The Taisho Era transfigured the Japanese character. New types abounded. Meet *mobo* and his sister (or lover) *moga* – modern boy and modern girl respectively, mobo in bell-bottom trousers, floppy tie, colored shirt and round-rimmed *roido* spectacles (named for American film star Harold Lloyd), moga having shed her "shapeless, unbecoming kimono" (the description is Tanizaki's) in favor of "Western clothes" that "accentuate every curve and hollow, give her body a brilliant surface and lively flowing lines." Mobo's hair was long, moga's short, sometimes boyishly short; sexuality was out in the open now and not to be hemmed in by simplistic old categories like "male" and "female."

Where did mobo and moga hang out? Most typically, in the new European-style cafés springing up here, there and just about all over the place, especially in Ginza,

Tokyo's little Europe. The first one opened in 1911 (coffeehouses, quite different, had been around for a generation); by 1939, nationwide, they numbered thirty-seven thousand. To the cafés streamed mobo and moga and all their various sub-species.

Disputation raged. This was not, by our standards, an educated generation – in 1920 less than half the population got beyond six years of compulsory schooling, with senior high school, let alone university, accessible to barely one percent of boys and the merest handful of girls. But Tokyo – population two million plus, one of the largest cities in the world – had one of the world's largest student populations. Literacy was widespread if not necessarily advanced; newspapers, magazines and books proliferated. The Communist Manifesto was translated in 1904; "Marx boys" and "Marx girls" pored over it, and the cafés were the backdrop for their fierce arguments over the fine points.

Not only Marx but "Dekansho" – Descartes, Kant and Schopenhauer – were the fashionable philosophical mentors of the day, and a lesson drawn from them was that the world was not merely to be accepted as given but recreated according to reason and justice. This implied varying degrees of action and commitment.

Most were content merely to read, debate and give themselves intellectual airs. Others – Bolsheviks, anarcho-syndicalists, radical feminists – were poised for action; for blood if necessary. The burgeoning industrial-capitalist society that surrounded them, with its machines, its factories, its appalling working conditions, its stark contrasts of grinding poverty and plutocratic wealth, was in their eyes irredeemably corrupt, debased, evil. They nurtured one hope for salvation: its utter destruction. From its ashes, they passionately believed, a new society would arise, more human, more compassionate, more fulfilling. Details were vague. Details could wait.

Relatively few were so grimly, deadly serious (not even the grimly serious ones were grimly serious all the time, and "free love" was no small part of the revolutionary ethos). More prosaic preoccupations were reflected in types who would seem very familiar to us today, however odd to their parents.

There were, first of all, the entrepreneurs, not only of heavy industry but of consumer goods. Prominent among them was the young electrician Konosuke Matsushita (1894-1989). In the early 1920s, a bicycle lamp consisted of a candle mounted in a glass-fronted box. The company that grew up around Matsushita's electric bicycle lamp became Matsushita Electric, then Panasonic, the world's largest manufacturer of consumer electronic products.

The nine-to-five company salaryman became numerous in this period, as did the newly-fledged "working girl," reveling in her financial independence. Department store clerk, train station ticket-seller, teacher, telephone operator, typist, elevator girl, nurse, writer, journalist, beautician – a Taisho woman might don any one of these identities.

Beautician? Japan's first Western-style hair salon opened in Mach 1923, six months before the Great Kanto Earthquake which, to not a few conservatives, was heaven's wrathful judgment on all this frivolous tinkering with native tradition. Chieko Yamano, twenty-seven years old and just back from training in New York, set up her parlor on the fourth floor of the Maru Building, Asia's largest structure at the time, just across the street from Tokyo Station. She employed twenty assistants, all in Western clothes and Western coiffeur. Conventional Japanese notions of feminine beauty, reflected in the languid poses of eighteenth- and nineteenth-century

163

ukiyo-e ("floating world" prints), were, if not out, clearly on the defensive. Not even the earthquake brought them much of a revival.

Or, a Taisho woman might become a *jokyu* (café waitress) serving coffee, whisky, wine and *hotto sandoitchi* (hot sandwiches), granting or withholding sexual favors as she saw fit. So numerous, so bright, charming and above all "modern" were the jokyu of Taisho – by 1936 there were some 112,000 of them – that, remove them from the scene and it dims perceptibly. Male customers fawned on them. Unlike all but the highest-ranking courtesans of the traditional licensed pleasure quarters, the jokyu was her own mistress, free to accept this homage or reject it. One jokyu is remembered for a pert rejoinder to a smitten mobo's eager advances. "*I* do the seducing," she snapped.

World War One "sent Europe to its knees and brought Japan to its feet," as historian Jeffrey Hanes put it. European and American industry's all-out mobilization for war created a vacuum that Japanese heavy industry, then in its infancy, rose to fill. The resulting war boom seeded Taisho's cultural and social ferment. There were fortunes to be made, and those quick to seize the opportunity made them, more or less irrespective of birth.

The salarymen who staffed the entrepreneurs' offices became the new middle class. Rougher types, male and female, kept the factories humming, suffering the attendant evils of long hours, low pay and an overall standard of living not much above brutality. "On those machines fall my tears," went a song lyric of the day.

Proletarian literature has its place in Taisho culture alongside less ephemeral literary celebrations of eros and the new freedom. "I was in the war and I can tell you that to spend eight hours down there in that mine was worse than twenty-four hours under enemy fire," says a mine worker in Mimei Ogawa's short story *The Handstand*, published in 1920. "What the hell," the miner continues, "we were risking our lives down there every day to make profits for the company. We all got together and were going to make a set of minimum demands for our safety. But we had an informer among us. Our plan leaked out and the company put a stop to it all."

The narrator listens to his talk and the truth dawns on him: "'A socialist,' I thought to myself." The narrator is wary but not unsympathetic. "I soon learned," he says, "that almost all the workers with whom I had now come to spend my time suffered to a greater or lesser extent from [a] sense of monotony. They were forever discussing possible ways of breaking the tedium of their lives." We see here the emergence of a strangely modern theme: tedium amid ceaseless activity.

Then there's Naomi – *Miss* Naomi, if you please – the sexual-predator moga protagonist of Tanizaki's novel *A Fool's Love* (1924), and she lives to this day as the personification of what came to be known – more approvingly than otherwise – as *Naomishugi* (Naomi-ism). The novel's narrator is a thirty-something salaryman – nothing special about him except a desire to adopt a child-wife he can mold to his own particular (though not perverse) tastes. Naomi, a starveling fifteen-year-old apprentice jokyu, appeals to him and, without much enthusiasm though with no repugnance either, accepts his overtures. His goal is to make her a woman who would meet Western standards of grace and style. He has money to spend and he spends it freely. For a time she is content to be his toy; then she discovers Western ballroom dancing. That sets her free, and off she dances, for better or for worse, into the brave new world of the liberated female, a species Japan had scarcely ever known before.

(2012)

Wet Sleeves: Love and Eros in Heian Japan

IT'S A STRANGE WORLD we're about to enter.

If I were the organizing type I would establish a "Heian Society." In flowing robes and ceremonial court caps, we would compose pun-laden poems simultaneously lamenting and celebrating the transience of life and beauty. The saké would flow, inhibitions dissolve, talk grow heated. What would we talk about? Why – about the things that matter: the seasons, the moon. Which season is more conducive to poetry – spring or autumn? Which moon – the misty one of spring, or the clear one of autumn – does more justice to the music of flute and koto?

Heian Japan: a world that lasted nearly four hundred years, from 794 to 1185, and yet "has disappeared from the face of the Earth far more completely than ancient Rome," as the historian Ivan Morris remarked. Not even ruins remain, only a voluminous literature; and the thought and ethical standards it reveals are as extinct as child sacrifice, though a lot less brutal.

"Disappeared," and yet it is ours to wander in at will, this vanished world, thanks to a voluminous literature which is its sole survival. Diaries, jottings, poems, and above all one very long, endlessly profound novel, *The Tale of Genji*, give us the keys to the kingdom – a kingdom as tiny as it is strange, for, humanity having been defined in such a way as to practically exclude the lower orders, its population is about ten thousand. These are "the good people," the cultivated, pampered aristocracy whose blithe indifference to anyone else's existence is one of its most conspicuous features.

Modern moralists have felt uncomfortable here. "Truth to say," wrote the British scholar W.G. Aston in 1899, "the laxity of morals which [*The Tale of Genji*] depicts is deplorable." Fortunately, though, "the language is almost invariably decent, and even refined, and we hardly ever meet with a phrase calculated to bring a blush to the cheek of a young person."

Refined language be damned, snapped Scottish historian James Murdoch, who in 1949 excoriated the Heian aristocracy as "an ever-pullulating brood of greedy, needy, frivolous dilettanti – as often as not foully licentious, utterly effeminate, incapable of any worthy achievement, but withal the polished exponents of high breeding and correct 'form'…"

I imagine reading that passage to Genji – how would he respond? With a smile? A shrug? A squint expressive of blank incomprehension? The latter, I think, as he confronted for the first time a possibility that would never in a million years have occurred to him otherwise: that there were, or could be, societies, or let's call them worlds, in which "morality" meant anything other than the behavior of which he was the supreme, most talented, most polished, most tasteful exemplar.

Any number of examples might be cited. This one comes from very early in the *Genji*, and the extraordinary thing about it is not the attempted seduction (rape, Murdoch would surely call it, not altogether unreasonably), but its failure. The woman's determined resistance is not, as it normally would be, for form's sake only. She really means it; she will have nothing to do with the shining Genji – not because she is a married woman, the wife of Genji's host, or because she resents Genji's highhanded assumption that the powerful longings aroused in him by an accidental glimpse of her are to be satisfied as a matter of right, or because she finds him unattractive (she most certainly does not), but because of her painful awareness of her own inferior social status relative to his. A look at how the episode plays out will give us an idea of what Heian lovemaking was like.

Genji at seventeen had been married for five years – unhappily, as was generally the case with first marriages arranged by families with an eye toward political advancement. A directional taboo (the requirement to avoid a certain direction so as not to disturb gods whose movements were predictable and charted) offered a convenient excuse for avoiding his wife's vicinity, and Genji, accompanied by a modest retinue of attendants and outrunners, inveigles an invitation from a provincial governor to spend the night at his estate. It is the elderly governor's young wife who has drawn Genji's attention.

She is the subject of talk as the saké cups are passed around, and Genji, waiting till the other revelers have passed out, sets off in search of her. Outside her pavilion he overhears her talking with her twelve-year-old brother; her attendant, he learns, is out for a bath; the brother (suborned earlier as Genji's spy) makes himself scarce, and she is alone. Genji slips inside. The lady gasps, but Genji hastens to soothe her:

"You are perfectly correct if you think me unable to control myself. But I wish you to know that I have been thinking of you for a long time. And the fact that I have finally found my opportunity and am taking advantage of it should show that my feelings are by no means shallow."

The narrator comments: "The little figure, pathetically fragile and as if on the point of expiring from the shock, seemed to him very beautiful."

"I promise you," Genji assures her, "that I will do nothing unseemly."

"She was so small," resumes the narrator, "that he lifted her easily." The attendant, back from the bath, is struck dumb with astonishment – partly feigned, no doubt. "Come for her in the morning," says Genji, sliding the doors shut.

The lady would seem to be at his mercy, but "naturally soft and pliant, she was suddenly firm." When at last she masters her weeping and is able to speak, the bitterness she expresses is not at Genji's presumptuousness, but at the lowly status (provincial governors were a despised class among the upper aristocracy) that makes her unworthy of such a brilliant suitor.

Episode after episode in the *Genji* remind us of the timeless truth that one culture's good taste is another culture's barbarism; one age's virtue, another's vice. There is Genji's first encounter with the lady Murasaki (not to be confused with the *Tale*'s author, Murasaki Shikibu) – the love of his love.

Murasaki. Her beauty is peerless, her gentleness unfailing, her quiet depths unsoundable. Genji often gave her grounds for unhappiness – such is fate! such is the nature of this flawed, evanescent world! – but never without repenting.

She was a child when he first saw her – a very young child. Genji, under the weather, had journeyed into the mountains to benefit from the healing powers of a sage who lived there. Feeling better as a result of the sage's spells and incantations, he goes for a stroll and glimpses, through a raised blind in a nun's hut, a little girl of ten. He is enchanted – not least by the child's uncanny likeness to his stepmother, whose own rumored resemblance to his late mother had kindled in him an adoration very much more than filial. Might he, he asks the nun, take charge of the child? "I have my reasons. You must believe me." The nun is surprised, though rather less so than you or I would be, or Murdoch. Genji's invoking of an apparent bond in a previous life as justification for his ardor strikes all concerned as plausible. Eventually he has his way, carrying the girl off with the somewhat hesitant connivance of her serving women, whose objections that her father will soon be coming for her are glibly dismissed. "I really do believe," says Genji, "that... my feelings for her are stronger than his." Hiding her in his palace, he keeps her as a kind of playmate until at last one day "he could not restrain himself. It would be a shock, of course."

That it was. Hours later Genji came in upon her as she lay in bed numb with horror, and the man known in his circle as the most exquisitely sensitive among the exquisitely sensitive addresses her with an insouciance that can only chill the modern reader: "What can be the trouble? I was hoping for a game of Go."

There is a strangely nebulous quality to Heian. At times you feel you can almost reach out and touch it, it seems so close – as when court lady Sei Shonagon grumbles in her *Pillow Book* of miscellaneous jottings at the unruly behavior of over-indulged four-year-olds, or when the anonymous author of *The Gossamer Years*, passing on a pilgrimage through a temple grove where speaking is forbidden, smiles (as this gloomy, tormented lady rarely does) at "my people, as such people will, gestur[ing] elaborately at one another to be quiet. They looked for all the world like gulping fish. It was irresistibly funny."

But Heian teases you with surface familiarity only to withdraw deeper and deeper into the shadows. So like us in their exclusive preoccupation with the peaceful and frivolous adornments of life, the Heian nobility nevertheless partook of the world very differently than we do. We may even say they partook of a different world altogether, for theirs – and this is perhaps the central fact of their attitude to life and love – is understood to be an illusion.

"How can she tell the dreaming from the waking?" murmured one of Genji's lesser ladies, dazzled by his wooing. This is more, very much more, than the cliché it might sound to us. All Heian literature, all Heian moral training, all Heian "philosophy," if such a word can apply to so fundamentally incurious a civilization, shared the underlying theme of the unreality of the physical world. To understand that things were so was to be civilized; to see beauty in the fact was to be potentially an artist; to have developed one's indifference to this illusory world to the point of willingness to cast it aside altogether was to be enlightened.

The Tale of Genji is considered a love story and its hero the age's greatest lover, but Genji's ultimate quest, what he most yearns for, is not love; it is sufficient detachment to "leave the world" – to take the tonsure and become a monk. Exorbitantly handsome and gifted, Genji must, despite his brilliant outward success, be

172

counted (as he counted himself) a failure, for the world, so delectably full of ladies, blossoms and moonlight, retains its hold on him to the bitter end.

A shadowy world begets a shadowy setting, and the setting in which the daily and nightly lives of Genji and his friends unfolds is sunk in perpetual twilight. Consider, first of all, that the women, objects of so much male striving, are most of the time invisible. They are thrice hidden: in darkness, behind curtains, and in clothing so voluminous that Edward Seidensticker, translator of both the *Genji* and *The Gossamer Years*, was moved to describe a typical Heian lady as "a shapeless and almost inert bundle of clothes surmounted by a spectral white face and masses of streaming hair." To add that she blackened her teeth and plucked her eyebrows, inking in a fresh pair just below the hairline, is to complete the portrait as we know it. Couples fall in love, and often consummate their love, never having seen one another. Sexual intercourse is not the ultimate intimacy but a prelude to it.

We are in a dream-world. Life is a dream – insubstantial, evanescent. Death is always near at hand, today's vigor no proof against tomorrow's wasting away. Without ever risking their lives in war, with no car accidents and plane crashes and terrorist bombs to worry about, the Heian nobles nonetheless felt themselves perpetually at death's door. Partly this is affectation, the cultivated pessimism of the age. But only partly. The constant references to life's fleeting nature are not mere cant. Epidemics were frequent, and medical care was in the hands of priests and exorcists. "I fear I have not long to live" is a recurring utterance. The fear was not entirely unreasonable.

Yes, Heian aristocrats feared death, and were not ashamed of their fear. On the contrary, so completely do they break the heroic mold that they display it almost eagerly, as a badge of the quality they prized as highly as their descendants would prize courage: sensitivity. Still, fear is not the only emotion to be considered in this context. Disease, feebleness and emaciation, we find, had peculiar charms of their own. Genji's Murasaki, fatally ill, was "as fragile as the shell of a locust" and the more beautiful for it: "Her skin was lovely, so white that it almost seemed iridescent, as if a light were shining through." Lady Fujitsubo, Genji's step-mother and, in spite of herself, his mistress (it was the child Murasaki's resemblance to her that first drew Genji's attention) was in physical pain and mental anguish, both brought on by Genji's persistent and abhorrent attentions. "'Might it be the end?' she was asking herself. Her profile was lovely beyond description."

"Few cultured societies in history," Ivan Morris remarks in *The World of the Shining Prince*, "can have been as tolerant about sexual relations as was the world of *The Tale of Genji*." From the *Genji* itself and from other literature of the period, we get the idea of a society sedentary to the point of motionlessness, venting its pent-up energy in the only arena available for physical activity: the bedroom. One needn't be a prude to be astonished at Heian promiscuity. Even our own day, promiscuous enough, pales beside it, if only because of the myriad other distractions available to us.

An unreal world presents little scope for action. Fighting there was none; governing, apparently, little more. The wheels of government did turn, after a fashion, which means someone must have been turning them, but whoever it was drew scant notice from the great writers of the day – partly because they were women and thus excluded from such work, partly also because the offices of government, though important for the emoluments and social status they conferred, were themselves unreal. Early eighth-century Japan, scarcely emerged from barbarism, had borrowed wholesale the complex administrative forms of what was then the most highly civilized society on earth. The Chinese forms remained intact long after the substance, irrelevant to local Japanese conditions, had drained out of them. Chinese-style offices and titles were sought and bestowed with great ceremony, but real power had long since shifted from them to the private offices of the supreme Fujiwara clan, whose de facto rule was extralegal but unchallengeable. No wonder, then, that Genji and his friends, high government officials all, had so much time on their hands, and no wonder also that on the rare occasions Sei Shonagon mentions government in her *Pillow Book*, it is in connection with some such thing as the granting of noble rank to a palace cat.

Cats were another Chinese import, which fact alone gave them an honored place among beasts. Murasaki Shikibu had no notice to spare for dogs, but she gave a cat a major role in a particularly dramatic *Genji* love story, one marking the onset of the hero's decline. Genji's elder brother, the retired Emperor Suzaku, is preparing to leave the world and become a monk, restrained only by concern for his youngest and favorite daughter, the thirteen-year-old Third Princess. Would Genji not oblige him by taking charge of the child? It would mean marrying her, and causing his beloved Murasaki heartache, but Murasaki had been so understanding over the years, so little given to the dread vice of jealousy; surely she will take this imposition too in stride, especially since Genji can assure her with perfect sincerity that he cares nothing for this latest and final addition to his ménage.

175

Indeed she is a hapless little thing – her calligraphy is a scandal, and that, said of a Heian lady, is as damning a denunciation as the gentle vocabulary of the times allowed. Calligraphy, even more than poetry, was the indispensible artistic accomplishment. Handwriting, not eyes, was the window of the soul. The girl's childish scrawl chills what little ardor Genji had mustered for his brother's sake. But a young man named Kashiwagi comes on the scene. He is the son of To no Chujo, Genji's best friend, and a friend of Genji's own son Yugiri. And one day while the young men are playing a kind of football on the grounds of Genji's sprawling estate – it is one of the very few scenes in all Heian literature involving physical exercise – the princess' cat breaks loose, disarranging the screens behind which the women are concealed and momentarily exposing the princess to Kashiwagi's awestruck gaze.

That moment seals Kashiwagi's doom. He is in love. Why? How? The conventional Buddhist explanation is invoked: it must be owing to a bond in another life. We come from other lives on our way to other lives – one more reason to hold this world at naught. Unable for now to get the girl, an increasingly disoriented Kashiwagi settles for the cat, managing to procure it and take it home with him. "Here," writes Richard Bowring in his 1988 study of the *Tale*, "attachment is taken to the extreme of fetishism, and the order of events suggests that the cat is actually to be preferred to the woman. The night Kashiwagi finally sleeps with the Princess he [dreams of] the cat rather than the girl..."

Consumed by guilt at having cuckolded Genji (a distant echo of Genji's guilt at having cuckolded his own father with Fujitsubo), Kashiwagi wastes away and dies without ever seeing the son he has sired. The son, Kaoru, will grow up to play a major role in the final phase of the novel, the embodiment of a rare and "reprehensible" amorous idiosyncrasy – the inability to either force himself on a woman who will not have him or transfer his affections at will to one who may.

Kashiwagi's illicit glimpse of the Princess is not to be interpreted as a glimpse of her naked. Far from it – the lady was swathed in layers of kimono. For all Ashton's talk of moral laxity, Murasaki Shikibu never so much as hints that beneath all the clothing are bodies. Her one other published work is a diary, which contains one curt reference to nudity: "Unforgettably horrible is the naked body. It really does not have the slightest charm."

Genji is not Heian's first idealized lover. That honor belongs to the poet Ariwara no Narihira, who lived a century before Genji's time and is the hero of a collection of poetic love adventures known as *The Tales of Ise*. Each of 125 chapters is a brief poem-studded episode that begins with the expression "In former times." "In former times a certain lascivious woman thought, 'I wish I could somehow meet a man who would show me affection!'" The trouble is, she is "a year short of a centenarian, hair disheveled and white." Never mind. Narihira will rise to the occasion. "It is a general rule in this world that men love some women but not others. Narihira did not make such distinctions."

Neither did Genji, and we catch a faint echo of Narihira in his uproarious romance with the aged Naishi. Hardly more than a boy at the time, and somewhat embarrassed at this unlikely coupling, Genji proceeds furtively. To no Chujo gets wind of it nevertheless, and in the spirit of fun insinuates himself as a rival. One night a disguised To no Chujo catches Genji and Naishi *in flagrante delicto.* "Silently and wrathfully, To no Chujo [brandished] a long sword." The adventure ends in hysterical laughter. It is one of only two scenes in the whole long tale in which a sword is drawn. (Genji, momentarily, is the other swordsman, his adversary an evil spirit.)

The Heian male is a soft, gentle creature. Sensitivity, not action, is what he was bred for. Men were moved to tears, not violence. The tears flow and flow. The sleeves that brush them away are never dry. Wet sleeves recur endlessly in the poems the lovers and friends exchange ("my sleeves are assaulted by wave upon wave"). Tears indicate anything from anger to delight. Delight itself is sorrowful, for does not beauty fade? Do not cherries bloom only to fall? Beauty was beautiful, of course, but also hauntingly impermanent, and if impermanence deepened beauty's poignancy, it also represents the central problem of Heian existence. It is to them what original sin, what evil, is to us. How is one to cope with this impermanent, insubstantial world?

The historian Murdoch, in his uncompromising disdain for the licentious mores of the time, seems to have missed a certain selfless, generous element in Genji's promiscuity. Born of a love almost preternatural in its intensity – his royal father was obsessed with a low-ranking court lady who shortly after Genji's birth was hounded to death by jealous rivals – Genji bestows his favors indiscriminately, and there is good as well as bad to be said for that. Donald Keene makes the point by suggesting a comparison to Don Juan, the classical Western exemplar of the indefatigable, irresistible lover. "My heart belongs to all women," says Moliere's Don,

178

but he cares nothing for them and thinks nothing of abandoning them once he has sated his lust. He is a conqueror of hearts who compares himself to Alexander. Genji surely never heard of Alexander – the Heian world stretched no farther than the Japanese and a select few Chinese classics could stretch it – and wouldn't have thought much of him if he had. Some of his ladies were far from beautiful and brought him little credit; he cherished them nonetheless. Even the pitifully thin, unfashionably dressed, red-nosed Safflower Lady, having once by accident drawn his attention, could count on his protection for life.

Central to the *Tale of Genji* is the hero's love for Murasaki. It is one of the few Heian loves that, its origins aside, seems, in its enduring power and its snug domesticity, almost normal to us – and yet, writes Bowring, to contemporaries "it would have undoubtedly seemed the most unrealistic, fictional aspect of the whole story." It is above all the romantic element in it that rings true to us, and rang false to them. "Romantic love can never become an ideal in a Buddhist world, because of the initial tagging of desire as original sin; such love is anathema to a Buddhist understanding of what constitutes reality." Love was not something one sought as the path to happiness; it was a pitfall one coped with while acquiring the inner discipline to leave the world.

Treacherous world! It would not consent to being left so easily. Is it any wonder that its snares were resented, and that love, the tightest snare of all, sometimes seems a veiled form of hate? A certain saintly recluse pronounces the truth that Genji appreciates only imperfectly: "Women are the problem, good for a moment of pleasure, offering nothing of substance. They are the seeds of turmoil..." And among the very few women in the *Tale* who steadfastly refuse to yield to the men who court them, one is regarded by her ubiquitous (and remarkably unservile) serving women as hexed, while another's resistance so puzzles her swain that he is driven in his frustration to muse that so impassioned a wooing as his would have caused any other lady to capitulate "however much she disliked a man." It was a woman's place, in short, to submit regardless of her feelings, so long as his were suitably intense, and then be blamed for cheating the man of his enlightenment.

We can only guess how women felt about this, for though almost all great Heian authors were female, they were curiously reticent on the subject. Our most significant clue is what they leave unsaid, and almost none of them – not the ebullient Sei Shonagon nor the pining *Gossamer* diarist nor the shy Murasaki Shikibu – so much as hints at sexual pleasure. Sei loves love's rituals, seasoned with exchanges of poetry and wit; Lady Gossamer wastes herself in yearning for a man whose company gives her little enough pleasure when he does show up. Murasaki Shikibu, of course, offers the world her Genji, the ideal lover, every woman's dream. He can indite a verse more beautifully, and intone it more feelingly, than anyone; he is handsome beyond description, and when he plucks a strain on the koto it achingly reverberates with the beauty and evanescence of the world. Yes, Genji is irresistible – but is he *sexually* irresistible? Does women's admiration of his good looks and artistic accomplishments amount to a desire to get into bed with him? Isn't sex rather the price a woman must pay for the pleasure of basking in his radiance? Isn't sex, in short, the price a woman must pay for love?

A younger member of Genji's inner circle broods, in the course of a personal crisis, over a world "altogether too wide and varied," bringing a smile to the lips of his twenty-first-century auditors because to us a narrower, less varied world than Heian is scarcely to be imagined. But his lament reminds us that, whatever the time and place, life is always just a little bit to much for the people living it. That thought brings us closer to the nobles of Heian, men and women who on first acquaintance tend as much to repel as to fascinate with their strangeness.

Perhaps no civilization in history ever invested so much of its psychological capital in love, was more alive to love's nuances, sought to tame and enjoy love's passions in ways more likely to strike us as bizarre. Bizarre and yet, after all, who's to say what's bizarre and what's normal? Won't people a thousand years from now, reading such evidence as remains of our love lives – of our lives in general – shake their heads over us as we shake ours over Heian?

Shake their heads they will, our future judges, and as they do they are unlikely to say of us what we can scarcely help saying of the Heian courtiers – that, bizarre or not, amoral or not, frivolous or not, at a time when most of the rest of the world was sunk in decline or barbarism, here were people imbued with a deep appreciation for, and gentle love of, beauty. It redeems many of their failings.

(2000)

The Ladies of the Battlefield

"AH, FOR SOME BOLD WARRIOR to match with, that Kiso might see how fine a death I can die!"

Tomoe Gozen was the prototypical Japanese female warrior. She had "long black hair and a fair complexion, and her face was lovely; moreover she was a fearless rider, whom neither the fiercest horse nor the roughest ground could dismay, and so dexterously did she handle sword and bow that she was a match for a thousand warriors, fit to meet either god or devil!"

A woman so dashing deserves to be better known. She figures, all too fleetingly, in the *Heike Monogatari*, the thirteenth-century chronicle of the twelfth-century Genpei War, the classic confrontation between the Taira and Minamoto military clans.

Minamoto won, which resulted in a power shift from Kyoto, the ancient capital, to the remote eastern encampment of Kamakura.

Tomoe Gozen was – what? the mistress? wife? servant? – the extant descriptions vary – of a Minamoto ally whose insubordination got him eliminated fairly early in the campaign. This was Minamoto Kiso Yoshinaka, who, surrounded and facing certain death, called Tomoe to him and said: "As you are a woman, it were better that you now make your escape."

"As you are a woman"! He scarcely knew her, obviously. But then, Japan has always scanted its female warriors. They seem at times almost an embarrassment, their very existence a blow to masculine pride. Bushido, the "Way of the Warrior," is "a teaching primarily for the masculine sex," wrote Inazo Nitobe in his book *Bushido* (1900), the classic English-language text on the subject.

But to return to Tomoe, bristling at Kiso's blindness to her finer qualities, "She drew aside her horse and waited," continues the *Heike Monogatari*. "Presently, Onda no Hachiro Moroshige of Musashi, a strong and valiant samurai, came riding up with thirty followers, and Tomoe, immediately dashing into them, flung herself upon Onda and, grappling with him, dragged him from his horse and pressed him calmly against the pommel of her saddle and cut off his head. Then, stripping off her armor, she fled away to the Eastern Provinces."

Nitobe's is the general view, but is it true? An old samurai tale, told by the novelist Ihara Saikaku (1642-93) in *Tales of Samurai Honor*, is apropos.

Samurai boy and samurai girl hear of each other and, sight unseen, fall in love. The parents' objections are overcome; they marry.

When their lord falls ill and dies, the young husband is bent on *seppuku* (ritual suicide) to prove his limitless loyalty. "Well, die bravely," says his wife. "I am a woman, and therefore weak and inconstant. After you're gone I'll look for another husband."

Embittered by this unexpected proof of worldly vanity, the husband is all the more determined to die. He commits glorious seppuku – and his wife follows him in death, having written, "At our final parting I spoke coldly, faithlessly, in order to anger my husband so he could die without regret at leaving me."

The moral of the story? Japanese men never knew their women.

The truth is, or seems to be, that women were every bit as imbued with the spirit of Bushido as men, little credit though they got for it. All Japanese women were warriors.

What was a Japanese warrior? "The idea most vital and essential to the samurai," wrote the seventeenth-century warrior Daidoji Yusan in *A Primer of Bushido*, is that of death." A warrior lived as though dead, because any moment he (or she) might be, by his (or her) own hand if not by an enemy's. "Think," said Yusan, "what a frail thing life is, especially the life of a samurai. This being so, you will come to consider every day of your life your last."

To that add one more concept, unconditional loyalty, and the ideology of Bushido is basically exhausted.

"Woman's surrender of herself to the good of her husband, home and family," wrote Nitobe, "was as willing and honorable as the man's self-surrender to the good of his lord and country. Self-renunciation… was the keynote of the loyalty of man as well as the domesticity of woman… In the ascending scale of service stood woman, who annihilated herself for man, that he might annihilate himself for the master, that he in turn might obey Heaven."

"The good of his lord and country" – but in fact, until modern times the concept of "country" was abstract to the point of nonexistence. Loyalty was purely personal. As for annihilation, there was that in profusion, notwithstanding the archipelago's security from hostile neighbors. Slaughter and self-slaughter mar the history of Japan – or brighten it, if you share the eerily necrophiliac *bushi* ethic – from the Genpei Wars until the early years of the long peace of the Edo Period (1603-1867).

185

"The archaeological evidence, meager though it is," writes historian Stephen Turnbull in *Samurai Women 1184-1877* (2010), "tantalizingly suggests a wider female involvement in battle than is implied by written accounts alone."

Armor and weapons have been found in the tombs of fourth-century female rulers. Do they support the historicity of the legendary Empress Jingu? They might – or might not; scholars disagree.

The eighth-century chronicle *Nihon Shoki* credits her with invading Korea in the third or fourth century AD – the dating (in fact the event itself) is uncertain. Pregnant but undeterred, she "took a stone, which she inserted in her loins, and prayed, saying, 'Let my delivery be in this land [Japan] on the day that I return after our enterprise is at an end."

And so at the head of her army she made the crossing, watched over by two guardian spirits, a "gentle spirit" and a "rough spirit." The invasion was successful, and the empress returned to give birth to the future Emperor Ojin, later deified as Hachiman, the Shinto god of war.

The gentle spirit and the rough spirit parted company. The Nara Period (710-784) and Heian Period (794-1185) were as uninterruptedly peaceful as history gets. During these centuries in which Japan acquired, assimilated and Japanified Chinese culture, the gentle spirit ruled unchallenged. The Genpei War marked its abdication or overthrow.

Now it was the rough spirit's turn. "Chaotic spirit" may be a better name. Historians despair of making sense of Japan's "Middle Ages," from the late twelfth century to the early seventeenth. Territorial lords led their unconditionally loyal, eagerly self-sacrificing samurai against neighboring territorial lords leading *their* unconditionally loyal, eagerly self-sacrificing samurai. The outcome in the fullness of time was the unification of Japan under the Tokugawa shoguns early in the Edo Period – but it took centuries of seemingly endless and purposeless slaughter and suicide.

The climax was the Sengoku Jidai (the "Age of the Country at War"), from the late fifteenth century to the late sixteenth. The whole spectacle looks from this distance like nothing so much as the pursuit of death as an ideal superior to life. If this environment bred women whose like it would be hard to find elsewhere, is it surprising?

What the sword was to a man – a weapon embodying his soul – the halberd-like *naginata* was to a woman. Picture, says Turnbull, "a cross between a sword and a spear with a curved blade rather than a straight one."

"When a *bushi* [warrior] woman married," writes martial-arts historian Ellis Amdur in *Women Warriors of Japan* (2002), "one of the possessions that she took to her husband's home was a naginata. Like the *daisho* [long and short swords] that her husband bore, the naginata was considered an emblem of her role in society. Practice with the naginata was a means of merging with the spirit of self-sacrifice, of connecting with the hallowed ideals of the warrior class."

"Young girls," Nitobe adds, "were trained to repress their feelings, to indurate their nerves, to manipulate weapons, especially the naginata" – not, he says, for service on the battlefield but rather, "With her weapon she guarded her personal sanctity with as much zeal as her husband did his master's."

That may be true, but Amdur, citing a sixteenth-century chronicle, shows us a bushi wife who, "appalled by the mass suicide of the surviving women and children in her husband's besieged castle" – a scene fairly typical of those years – "armed herself and led eighty-three soldiers against the enemy, 'whirling her naginata like a waterwheel.'"

One thing is certain: if chivalry is conspicuously absent from the Japanese tradition, there's a reason. It wouldn't have worked.

The legendary ancient British King Arthur and his Knights of the Round Table are said to have sworn an oath, prototype of the Western knightly ideal of chivalry, "to fight only in just causes, at all times to be merciful, and at all times to put the service of ladies foremost." There was no such ideal in old Japan, little that we today would recognize as either justice or mercy, let alone service to ladies. Still, perhaps even in Japan there is an instinctive masculine deference to – or maybe it is simply contempt for – perceived feminine weakness.

Turnbull, describing an event much later in time than the Sengoku Jidai but reminiscent of it in spirit, says of the siege by the forces of the Meiji Imperial Restoration of 1867 against the last unreconciled Tokugawa loyalists, women among them, at Aizu Castle in today's Fukushima Prefecture, "What followed was a bloody encounter that would have been more in keeping with the story of Tomoe Gozen rather than the year 1868. When the Imperial troops realized that they were facing women the cry went up to take them alive, but holding their fire meant that the women were soon upon them. Nakano Takeko" – of whom more shortly – "killed five or six men with her naginata before being shot dead."

Nitobe mentions another weapon handled by bushi women – again, not on the battlefield, he says, for he hardly acknowledged women's presence there. "Girls," he says, "when they reached womanhood, were presented with *kaiken* [dirks] which might be directed to the bosom of their assailants, or, if advisable, to their own… When a Japanese maiden saw her chastity menaced, she did not wait for her father's dagger. Her own weapon lay always in her bosom. It was a disgrace to her not to know the proper way in which she had to perpetrate self-destruction."

Tomoe Gozen, according to one of several versions of her legend, became a nun and lived to the ripe old age of ninety-one after she "fled away to the Eastern Provinces." This, if true, is a striking exception to the general rule that life in a state of nature or warfare is "nasty, brutish and short," as Thomas Hobbes expressed it for the West – or fleeting like cherry blossoms, as Japanese tradition has it. The difference in emphasis is significant: the West deplores the truncated life; Japan beautifies it.

Short-lived male Japanese warriors are accorded literary immortality, their deeds sung by future ages. Of how many women can that be said? How many of them are household names? Is Hangaku Gozen one? Sakasai Tomohime? Myorin-ni? The aforementioned Nakano Takeko of Aizu?

They span Japan's bellicose centuries, from Hangaku (twelfth century) to Nakano (nineteenth). The two women in between are of the Sengoku Jidai, defenders to the death of besieged castles – two among a great many, for castle defense was a woman's responsibility when the lord was off fighting, as he almost always was in those years.

189

The apparent absence in these people of the faintest fear under the most fearful conditions, the total absence – or suppression? – of the instinctive, animal – and therefore subhuman? – will to live, makes them shining exemplars of the Way of the Warrior, and, to non-practitioners of that Way, more than a little chilling. The death of Sakasai Tomohime was especially remarkable. Her husband slain, the enemy triumphant, she cut down with her naginata a bronze signal bell and, weighted with it, plunged into the castle moat to drown. The year was 1536. She was nineteen.

Hangaku and Nakano, seven centuries apart, have much in common; they would have understood one another. They are linked by the naginata they wielded, by their common role as castle defenders (though a twelfth-century castle wasn't much of a stronghold), by the state of rebellion in which they found themselves, by their unswerving loyalty to a clan, and by their innocence of any abstract ideal other than loyalty.

In Hangaku's case that last was natural; in Nakano's it is more to be wondered at. When Hangaku's clan rebelled against the Minamoto shogunate in 1189, it was a naked power struggle. "While archers [kept] up covering fire from the tower above the gate," writes Turnbull, "Hangaku Gozen [rode] into action, swinging her naginata." Like Tomoe, her near contemporary, she is a rare survivor. Wounded and captured, she was prevented from committing seppuku by an enemy warrior who sought her as a bride. This was a new twist; her physical charms were said to be meager. Her subsequent marriage says something about the eros of raw courage, the beauty of unsullied bravery, in times such as hers.

Though very late in Japan's heroic tradition, "Aizu's women," writes Turnbull, "were the most authentic women warriors in the whole of Japanese history." Why

190

they are more "authentic" than others is not clear, but certainly they are no less so.

The Aizu clan, a branch of the Tokugawa from around the city of Aizu-Wakamatsu in present-day Fukushima Prefecture, preferred extinction to an Imperial Restoration at the expense of the Tokugawa shogunate. The result was the Boshin War – Japan's first, perhaps, in which abstract principles, rather than mere territorial aggrandizement, were at stake.

The new Meiji regime that took power in 1868 stood for modernization, industrialization and Westernization – if only to defeat the encroaching Western "barbarians" at their own game. Tokugawa meant seclusion, stagnation, tradition. But this was beside the point for Aizu's defenders, and for Nakano Takeko among them as she charged the guns of the Imperial forces with her naginata. Loyalty and the chance to die beautifully were their sole inspiration. We gather as much from the death poem left by another female defender of the besieged castle:

> *Each time I die and am reborn in the world*
> *I wish to return as a stalwart warrior.*

Struck down by a bullet in the chest, Nakano with her dying breath ordered her sister Yuko to cut off her head and save it from the enemy. She was twenty-one. Her head was buried under a tree in a temple courtyard.

The Boshin War, in Turnbull's view, marks the end of the age of the female warrior: "Just as the elite samurai class gave way to the conscript army of the modernizing Meiji government, so did women warriors give way to men, and Japan's modern wars, from the Sino-Japanese War [1894-5] to World War Two, were all-male affairs."

Were they really? "The whole Japanese race was at war" – that's how World War Two looked to Tetsuko Tanaka. She was a high school student, but "our education became mostly volunteer work" – in her case, making paper for balloon bombs designed to wreak havoc in the United States. Her recollections, and those of several older women who deserve to be considered World War Two warriors, on or off the battlefield, are included in *Japan at War: An Oral History*, by Haruko Taya Cook and Theodore F. Cook (1992).

Tanaka is quite right – the martial spirit raged nationwide. Typical are the experience and the feelings of Toki Tanaka (no relation), a young farm wife at the time, not naturally bellicose, who recalls, "As the war dragged on… we practiced with bamboo spears on the school ground under the blazing hot sun. Some fainted because of the heat. Men made the spears for us and hung up dolls made of straw, shaped like men… But when I thought about my husband's hardship at the front, doing that much seemed natural."

Tetsuko Tanaka was of samurai stock: "My grandmother used to tell me, 'You must behave like the daughter of a warrior family.' I was always conscious of that." The balloon bombs were Japan's "secret weapon." Some nine thousand were launched, to little effect as it turned out. The girls at Tanaka's school in Yamaguchi Prefecture threw themselves into the work, desiring only to be worked harder: "We addressed a petition to our principal, pledging ourselves in blood. One of the girls who lived near the school rushed home to get a razor so we could cut our fingers to write in blood, 'Please let us serve the nation.'"

192

"We only learned some forty years later," she said, "that the balloon bombs we made actually reached America. They started a few forest fires and inflicted some casualties, among them children... When I heard that I was stunned."

Kikuko Miyagi was a student nurse serving on the battlefields of Okinawa. Mobilized in February 1945, "I assured Father and Mother I would win the Imperial Order of the Rising Sun, eighth class, and be enshrined at Yasukuni. Father was a country schoolteacher. He said, 'I didn't bring you up to the age of sixteen to die!' I thought he was a traitor to say such a thing."

The horrors she endured during the awful Battle of Okinawa are beyond the scope of this story. The American forces closed in. "For the first time, we heard the voice of the enemy: 'We have food! We'll rescue you!' They actually did!" The Americans weren't demons after all. "So what we had been taught robbed us of life. I can never forgive what education did to us!"

Would the heroines of Bushido say the same of their education if they could see life from today's standpoint? Or would modern times, rooted in the pursuit of long life and personal happiness, seem to them hopelessly depraved and decadent?

(2011)

"Soothing Liquor, Smiling Liquor": Japan Under the Influence

"A CIVILIZATION STANDS or falls," observed essayist Kenichi Yoshida, "by the degree to which drink has entered the lives of its people, and from that point of view Japan must rank very high among the civilizations of the world."

It must indeed. The first foreigners ever to record observations of the Japanese – Chinese envoys of the third century AD – noted, "They are much given to strong drink." Traces on prehistoric pottery suggest fruit-brewing as early as the Jomon Period (c.12,000 BC-c.300 BC). The history we're embarked on is therefore a very long one – no end of parties to crash!

Chronological order is for the birds, for the sober, for pedants – anyone you like; not for us. The fourteenth century beckons – a whimsical choice of beginnings, admittedly – but aren't all beginnings whimsical?

The notable event of the fourteenth century was the Kenmu Restoration, a doomed attempt by Emperor Go-Daigo in Kyoto, the ancient capital, to wrest real, as opposed to merely ceremonial, power from the shogunate, the regime of military "eastern barbarians" in Kamakura.

Drink and conspiracy go hand in hand – a *very* old story, that, of which more in a moment. The *Taiheiki*, a contemporary narrative, describes attempts by a certain Lord Suketomo, high in the ranks of the Imperial loyalists, to sound out two men "renowned for their valor" but of uncertain allegiance. Whose side were they on – the Emperor's, or the Kamakura shogun's?

"In diverse ways Lord Suketomo drew near to these," the *Taiheiki* reports, "until the bonds of his friendship with them waxed strong. And it came to pass that Suketomo made a group, called by the name of the Band of Roisterers, thinking thereby to search their hearts to the bottom...

"Most amazing were the aspects of these men's parties and meetings! In offering wine, they made no distinction of degree between the high and the low. Likewise, men cast off their caps and loosened their top hair, while monks showed their persons in white undergarments without their gowns. The wine was served by more than twenty maidens of sixteen or seventeen years, clear-skinned and superior in face and figure, through whose unlined robes of raw silk the snowy white skin gleamed fresh as lotus blossoms.

"The guests sported and danced and recited verses. Yet all the while they took counsel together, how they might strike down the eastern barbarians." And so Suketomo had his answer.

Drink and conspiracy – the threads of that tale take us all the way back to the mythological age of the gods. Susano'o, the storm god, best known for his atrocious behavior towards his sister the sun goddess, turns out to be not all bad – he rescues a maiden from a fearful dragon about to consume her. How does he do it? With saké, which he had prepared in advance. The dragon "had an eight-forked head and an eight-forked tail," says the eighth-century *Nihon Shoki*. "As it crawled it extended over a space of eight hills and eight valleys. Now when it

196

came and found the saké, each head drank up one tub, and it became drunken and fell asleep."

The maiden's rescue was assured. Long, long afterward, the comic haiku poet Karai Senryu (1718-90) drew a moral from the story:

Even in the time of the gods
they needed wine to deceive others.

"There came over [to Japan]... a man who knew how to distil liquor," another eighth-century chronicle, the *Kojiki*, tells us. The man was a Korean, Susukori by name.

"So this Susukori distilled some great august liquor, and presented it to the heavenly sovereign" – the Emperor Ojin, roughly datable to the fourth century AD – "who, excited with the great august liquor that had been presented to him, sang, 'I have become intoxicated with the august liquor distilled by Susukori. I have become intoxicated with the soothing liquor, with the smiling liquor.'"

Not much is known of Emperor Ojin (he is vaguely associated with an invasion of Korea), but evidently he knew how to enjoy himself. The *Nihon Shoki* records a subject people known as the Kuzu, mountain folk of the remote Kii Peninsula, coming to Ojin's court to present "thick saké" and singing,

We have brewed the fine great liquor:
See how good it is –
Come, partake, down it with joy, our father.

197

Why "thick" saké? The answer may disgust a modern drinker. The earliest saké was termed *kuchikami no saké* – literally, "chewing-in-the-mouth saké." "This saké," writes Hiroshi Kondo in *Saké: A Drinker's Guide*, "was made by chewing rice, chestnuts or millet and then spitting the wad into a large wooden tub where it was allowed to brew for several days." Enzymes in saliva convert starch into alcohol, and the world's problems no longer seem so intractable after all.

Ritualized, the chewing and spitting became, along with drinking, part of Shinto religious festivals. As a rule, says Kondo, "only young virgin were allowed to chew the rice. These virgins were considered mediums of the gods, and the saké they produced was called *bijinshu*, or 'beautiful woman saké."

It was more solid than liquid, and was eaten rather than drunk – with "chopsticks joined at the top," writes Kondo, "like pincers."

Refinement proceeded slowly, over centuries. Thick saké grew thinner, ultimately turning liquid. Black saké turned white and finally transparent – "a jeweled broom that sweeps away all care," as the proverb has it. The holiest of men, and others not so holy, have sung its praises:

"If I could but be happy in this life,/ what should I care if in the next/ I became a bird or a worm!" – Otomo no Tabito (665-731) in one of his "thirteen poems in praise of saké.

"Today gloriously drunk/ we no longer know the meaning of unhappiness" – Zen hermit-monk-poet Ryokan (1758-1831).

"Living only for the moment... singing songs, drinking saké, caressing each other, just drifting, drifting..." – Asai Ryoi (1612-91), satirical novelist and Buddhist priest.

"The sky at sunset – / a cup of saké/ would taste so good!"
– Taneda Santoka, Zen monk, haiku poet and itinerant beggar (1882-1940).

"The complexity of qualities that go to make good saké suffices to give one the illusion that a universe of good things surrounds one while doing nothing but tasting from a cup."
–essayist Kenichi Yoshida (1912-77), whom we've already met.

Civilized society is a precarious arrangement, beneficial perhaps but not natural. It goes against the grain. Deep down we'd rather be savage.

Few premodern civilizations are without some form of ritual savagery. The ancient Greeks had their drunken Dionysian revels, the Romans their Saturnalia, medieval Europe its Feasts of Fools. Japan has its local *matsuri* (festivals); has them still, in fact: "The noise and confusion, expressions of hostility, and orgiastic behavior we can still observe today in many matsuri, would be unthinkable in ordinary time," wrote historian Herbert Plutschow in *Matsuri: The Festivals of Japan* (1995).

Sexual license is one characteristic feature, violence another, and drunkenness, of course, a third – it's hard to lose your senses without being drunk. Plutschow quotes a description from the 1950s of Kyoto's Kurama Fire Festival: "People were shouting, singing, quarreling; bare shoulders, bare chests, bare buttocks, ecstatic faces, intoxicated faces, faces in pain…"

That's us; and civilization has long known the wisdom of allowing those bottled-up energies some channeled release.

Imagine life without alcohol. Civilization would drive us mad: we're only human, after all.

The Mesopotamians and Egyptians five thousand years ago had beer; the ancient Greeks had wine; East Asians, fortunately, stumbled upon saké. It seems to have been a fortuitous discovery. Kondo cites an eighth-century Japanese document relating "how a cask of steamed rice was accidentally left uncovered. The owner found to his horror that the rice had molded... Several day later he discovered that the cask of spoiled rice had been transformed into a cask of delicious saké."

What else would a primitive mind see in that but the work of the gods? The link between intoxication and religious elevation seems natural and inevitable.

Japan's is a culture of rules, etiquette, decorum, control, self-control. "If you live on an island you can't be one," art critic Robert Hughes observed of the Japanese in the American news magazine *Time* in 1983. No Japanese is an island. What, then? A cog in a machine? A note in a symphony? A cell in the body politic? Anyway, a small part of an immense whole. "The entire country," wrote historian Hiroshi Watanabe in *A History of Political Thought, 1600-1901* (2010), "was a vast chain of those who were bowed to and those who did the bowing."

Thank the myriad gods for saké. In drink is liberation; in drunkenness, absolution. Short of murder, you can get away with anything when drunk. When drunk – and only then – you almost *can* be an island.

"When inebriated, society dictates, men are not accountable for their actions," wrote journalist Samantha Culp in a feature titled *Poor Man's Geisha* in the Hong Kong newspaper *The Standard* (2006), following a brief stint as a hostess in central Tokyo's Ginza district – "whether those [actions] entail attempting to squeeze a hostess' thigh or puking and then passing out on a subway platform."

"A man who creates a ruckus on a late-night binge," wrote Kondo in the *Drinker's Guide*, "may, when apprehended and cooled off, be asked to write a formal letter of apology. He will begin, 'I was drinking saké...' Few people in Japan would need to hear more."

True now, true a thousand years ago. Here, in Murasaki Shikibu's classic eleventh-century novel *The Tale of Genji*, is a highly dignified courtier assiduously wooing a young lady: "He was now quite open in his suit. Pretending to be hopelessly drunk, he was very amusing indeed as he gamboled about all willow-like with a spray of wisteria in his cap."

Interesting that he was only pretending. The literature of the Heian Period (794-1185) records much drinking but surprisingly little "hopeless" drunkenness. Decorum was stretched, not shattered. A characteristic entertainment of the day was the "winding water banquet." Saké cups were set afloat on the artificial streams that typically adorned the grounds of nobles' mansions, each guest in turn taking a cup as it floated by, sipping from it, and reciting a verse. One imagines the verses growing freer and more ribald as the night wore on – but decorum was stretched, not shattered.

Saké-brewing was Japan's first commercial enterprise. Associated in Heian times and earlier exclusively with shrine and court, it passed into entrepreneurial hands in the early years of the Kamakura shogunate (1192-1333).

Kamakura is known mainly for inaugurating Japan's stern military tradition, but it has another claim to fame: Its stable currency fostered a commercial spirit.

"Descendants of the families that had run the saké breweries of the court," Kondo explains, "now sought permission from the new government to establish themselves as independent brewers, or formed guilds associating themselves with powerful temples and shrines and going into business under their protection."

Fortunes were made. Warriors were not supposed to be drinkers, but they proved open to temptation after all. Kyoto's culture, despised in the Kamakura shogunate's early years as effete, gradually took hold. Battle-hardened samurai became Kyotoized in spite of themselves.

By the fourteenth century, says Kondo, there were 342 saké brewers in Kyoto alone, Kamakura being a prime market. Fierce competition and increasingly sophisticated consumer tastes generated vast improvements in brewing techniques. Something like what came to be known as pasteurization seems to have been developed by saké brewers in Nara as early as 1599. The Kansai region of western Honshu produced the best sakés, thanks to its fortuitous combination of pure water and high-quality rice.

The prime brewing season was during the cold months. It was a labor-intensive process. Seasonally idled farmers and fishermen flocked to the saké breweries, their muscles in acute demand. Then, from the early seventeenth century, the construction and swelling population of Edo (present-day Tokyo) created a huge new market.

An indication of how rich the major brewers grew is the intensity of the hatred they inspired in times of famine and upheaval. Rioting peasants went for the rice brokers and saké brewers first. A record survives of the interrogation of a peasant leader named Tatsuzo following an 1836 uprising in Mikawa Province (present-day Aichi Prefecture). It is cited in a 1994 essay by Makoto Takeuchi, suggestively titled *Festivals and Fights: The Law and the People of Edo*:

"Interrogating officer: You break into the households of respected merchants, smash apart casks of saké. You call that a festival to rectify the world?

"Tatsuzo: To hoard rice, to take this rice that sustains us in this transient life and squander it in making saké – that is what causes suffering for so many people."

The Japanese, it is said, are not good drinkers. The problem is genetic. Deficient in a certain enzyme that helps metabolize alcohol, some fifty percent of Japanese – and a similar proportion of north Asians generally – apparently suffer from what is informally known as Asian glow. The technical term is Alcohol Flush Reaction. The symptoms are flushed face, dizziness, nausea and a tendency to get maybe a bit more obnoxious a bit more quickly than drinkers with more alcohol-friendly chromosomes.

The syndrome is well documented and seems authentic, but the essayist Yoshida, for one, has no time for it – or for drinkers who can't hold their liquor. He acknowledges only those who can, those who can't being a disgrace to the bars, geisha houses or hostess establishments they frequent. They have no place in an urbane and witty writer's essays.

"In the West," Yoshida says, speaking of alcohol's role in commerce circa 1975, "businessmen drink after the deal has been done. In Japan they indulge during and after the deal. Any restaurant of any size advertises rooms for 'business talks' – and first they mellow themselves before getting down to the sordid details, the ancient wisdom of the race having taught them that drinking really does make men mellow and, in moderation, stimulates the brain.

"If talks come to a satisfactory conclusion, they see no reason to stop drinking and go home. If they do not, they go on drinking in the hope that some way out of the difficulties will be found in their cups."

Culp, the journalist who briefly turned bar hostess to research *Poor Man's Geisha*, may be less witty, or less tolerant, or more realistic; or else her more acerbic view may reflect changes that occurred in the course of the thirty years that separate her from Yoshida.

She writes, "Drinking is a huge part of the hostess world, and of Japanese business culture itself. In a country where a staggering percentage of the male populace staggers home each night, 'alcoholism' is hard to define. Hostess bars have an important role to play in this culture that requires obligatory drinking with colleagues after work, and getting wasted with partners to seal a business deal. Drinking comes to signify trust, relaxation and a certain absolution from adult responsibility.

"The fact that the female manager of such a club is called *mama-san*," she adds tartly, "is no coincidence."

The hostess bar is a modern offshoot of the old licensed pleasure quarters, to which a fleeting visit now seems in order. An early twentieth-century English-language guidebook written by one T. Fujimoto, cited in *Yoshiwara: Geishas, Courtesans and the Pleasure Quarters of Old Tokyo* by Stephen and Ethel Longstreet (1970), notes, "The hostess and maids of the house receive you very hospitably and lead you to a room upstairs... Everything in the room makes you comfortable. A clever-looking maid comes up with a tea-set and serves you tea and cakes, then asks you whether you want to take saké and some dishes, hire geisha and jesters.. In another room the samisen is heard... Lots of saké and good food produce in the guest an amorous nature."

Of course they do – but is that a good thing? "The romance of the Japanese tea house in these days is an absolute myth," fumes Clement Scott, a Victorian-era British traveler and author whom the Longstreets also quote. "At the gate of a tea house... stood the funny but inevitable little Japanese girls, gaily bowing and smirking... asking the 'honorable' gentlemen to come in and rest and laugh and chaff with them and take just one cup of their 'honorable' tea. Tea in a modern Japanese tea house in these days of civilization means, I fear, whisky with or without water... Peach blossoms may surround it [the tea house], but the almond-eyed maidens are employed here to tempt the traveler to drink and romp."

That, the alert reader will have noticed, is our first reference to an alcoholic beverage other than saké. For a thousand years and more, "drinking" in Japan meant, almost exclusively, though not quite, drinking saké. The exception was *shochu*. A fragment of graffiti inscribed on a roof beam of the Koriyama Hachiman Shrine in Kagoshima is attributed to two carpenters working there in 1559: "The high priest was so stingy he never once gave us shochu to drink. What a nuisance!"

Relatively refined nowadays, shochu, distilled mainly from sweet potatoes, was a rough tipple, scarcely better

205

than a gargle, too coarse to enter the literature. And so in the popular imagination if not in actual fact, "drinking" and "saké" were synonymous until Japan's mid-nineteenth-century opening to the West. That threw the scene wide open, with results describable as invigorating or disastrous, depending on point of view.

What is indisputable is that the "soothing liquor, smiling liquor" celebrated all those misty ages ago by Emperor Ojin has been in sad popular decline ever since, though it's said very lately to be on the cusp of a revival. Yoshida's businessmen were as likely to be drinking beer, wine or whisky as saké; Culp's clients much more so.

Yoshida celebrates the democratic nature of saké: "In the West, people drink champagne in marble halls and gin in cheap bars. In Japan the same saké is drunk in palatial chambers... and in small stalls in streets frequented by draymen."

True, and yet – as the novelist Nagai Kafu (1879-1959) grumbles in *Two Days in Chicago* (1910), a youthful short story describing a convivial American family dinner spiced with lively banter, delightful music and wine served in tasteful moderation – "Think of the way I was brought up at home, by a father whose warm human blood had been chilled by the Confucian classics and a mother restrained by treatises on womanly virtue and behavior. No room for music and laughter. My father would drink with his friends till past midnight and assail my mother, already exhausted from the day's chores, for the way the saké was warmed or the food cooked..."

"Even dignified men [under the influence] suddenly turn into lunatics and behave idiotically," complained the fourteenth-century Buddhist priest Yoshida no Kenko in

Grasses of Idleness (1330-32). "The victim's head aches even the following day, and he lies abed, groaning, unable to eat, unable to recall what happened the day before, as if everything had taken place in a previous incarnation."

We all know the feeling – but, adds Kenko, sacrificing consistency to higher truth, "On a moonlit night, a morning after a snowfall, or under the cherry blossoms, it adds to our pleasure if, while chatting at our ease, we bring forth the wine cups."

It does, doesn't it?

(2013)

The Fish Tree

ONCE UPON A TIME there was a child who, being a child, simply didn't know what to make of himself. "Look," said his mother. "I brought the sun out for you. Go out and play."

"With the sun?"

"Why not with the sun?"

"Mom?"

"Yes, child. Yes, dearest."

"Am I the only child in the world?"

"What?"

"Don't be angry."

"I'm not angry. But… honestly, the way you talk sometimes!"

The child went outside. The sun was out, as his mother had said, but there were clouds in the sky too, sullen clouds, angry clouds; the sun had better look out if it didn't want to get eaten. One cloud, in fact, and by no means the biggest, had already bitten into a small corner of it, and others were crowding round with no very kindly intent. The child shut his eyes as tightly as he could. He clenched his lips and his little fists. Such strength as he had he would gladly give to the sun, but it was no use. He opened his eyes to find it gone, swallowed.

"You there!" cried the old man. "Come out of there! Come out I say! What are you doing here?"

The child made no answer. It was raining, a slow, steady drizzle, and he was quite wet. His hair, long, thick and black, was soaked. His clothes clung to his skin. He had evidently been out in the rain a long time. Seeing an open shed, he had made for it, but the old man had spotted him and was furious at being trespassed upon. "Are you a deaf-mute, or what? Answer me!"

Still the child remained silent, and yet it was not terror that stopped his tongue, that much was clear. He regarded the old man with mild curiosity, and the slight smile playing about his lips suggested he found him amusing rather than frightening. Even when the old man, his aged face twisted with rage, raised a hand as though to strike him, the child did not shrink and seemed quite oblivious to the danger he was in. The old man's hand dropped. "Who are you?" he asked, his anger giving way to a kind of wounded bewilderment.

"It's raining," was the child's reply.

"Yes. Yes, it is," said the old man.

"You must be very old," said the child.

"Yes indeed. Very old indeed. Tell me who you are and where you come from."

"I'm a child," said the child.

"What's your name?"

"I don't know."

"You don't know?"

"I haven't given myself a name yet."

"See here, my boy, if you – "

"I'm hungry."

"What business is that of mine?"

"What?"

"You can starve to death for all I care! Is that clear enough for you?"

"What's death?"

210

"What are you doing here? Where do you come from? Answer me!"

"I come from heaven, my mom says."

"Well that's where you can go back to."

The rain was heavier now. The man turned towards the house. The child followed.

"Do you live here all alone?"

"Yes, alone. Of course, alone."

There was a crack of thunder.

"Could I have a hot bath, do you think? I'm very wet."

There was no help for it. You can't send a child out into a storm like that. "A hot bath. His little highness wants a hot bath. His diminutive majesty desires to bathe." Grumbling, the old man went off to prepare the bath, while the child, as though quite at home, went into the kitchen and opened the refrigerator.

"You don't speak the accent of these parts," said the old man. The child, bathed and refreshed, his appetite for the moment sated, looked quite comical in a white shirt of the old man's, which hung down past his knees and was belted at the waist by one of the old man's neck ties, but it was the best that could be done under the circumstances and the child was quite content.

"Will you teach it to me?"

"What, the accent? Of course, if you want me to, though I think yours is rather nicer. Where do you come from?"

"From the village."

"What village?"

"Well, the village. My daddy is the mayor."

211

"Is he, now! If you're the mayor's son you must know the name of the village! Or maybe" – he guffawed, his laugh scarcely distinguishable from coughing – "maybe you haven't given it one yet! Eh?"

"Am I the only child in the world?"

"Are you the – " The old man gaped at the child. He shook his head. "One doesn't know quite how to take you! Do you know – this thought occurs to me now: Maybe it's not just your accent that's different, maybe your language is too, and though we seem to understand each other we don't really, and words that sound the same actually have completely different meanings in your village and in mine. What do you think now, eh? Is that possible?"

"Once upon a time there was a child, and he was the only child in the world."

"What's that?"

"I made it up. Is this a village?"

"Of course it's a village. What else would it be?"

"Are there any children in it?"

"How would I know? I tend my garden and mind my business. Let other people mind theirs."

"There are no children in my village. They had to close the school."

"That's too bad."

"I'm sleepy."

"Sleepy, are you? Well, I guess you would be, after your long journey. But where can we put you? There's only one bed, mine. That's always been enough. Suddenly it isn't. Hm. Listen, won't your people come looking for you? They'll call the police and there'll be no end of bother! All right, all right, here's what we'll do. Come. Aaagh, what a nuisance!"

From a cupboard in the hall the old man took down some bath towels, which he carried to a corner of the kitchen and arranged as best he could into a kind of bed.

"Will this do? I'm sure your little highness is used to better, but... here, you can use this towel as a pillow, and this one as a blanket. First thing tomorrow we'll have to – " He broke off; the child was already sound asleep.

Dusk deepened slowly into night. The child slept on, but it was otherwise with the old man. For the first time ever there was an alien presence in his house, and though that presence was a mere child, sound asleep in another room and therefore invisible to him, his solitude had been invaded; he felt it; it disturbed him and kept him awake. The driving rain of a few hours before had eased; its pounding on the roof was less urgent, almost musical; he might have enjoyed it, perhaps, under other circumstances. "What do I have to do with children? And such a strange child! 'Am I the only child in the world?' How old would he be, I wonder? Five? Six? He's missing a front tooth. Imagine, a little mite of six wandering off all by himself... his parents will be frantic! His father the mayor of the village!" He tensed suddenly. An unfamiliar noise – police sirens? He imagined police cars converging on his house in force, lights flashing, sirens blaring... They'd snatch the child and arrest him, the old man, as a child thief; they'd throw him in prison and laugh as he protested his innocence! "How can you be innocent?" they'd say. "You've been arrested, haven't you?"

Should he contact the police himself? Maybe that was the thing to do. He'd report that a child had turned up in his shed in the storm, that he'd fed the child and sheltered him out of pity, that he didn't know who he was, and so on. That way there'd be no concealment, or apparent concealment; there'd be nothing to suspect him of, and the child would be returned immediately and safely – the sooner the better – to his people, to the mayor of whatever village it was, and that would be that. Yes, that was the thing to do, that was the wisest course.

What time would it be? There were no watches or clocks in the house; no calendar either. What need had he of them? The sun told him everything he needed to know – when to sleep, when to rise, when to plant his seeds, when to harvest. The nights he slept through, so the question of whether it was two o'clock in the morning or four o'clock in the morning never arose. Still, the outside world, he knew, ran on clock time; in dealing with it you needed to know what day and hour and minute of what month and year it was. Besides, it was raining. He had no telephone of course, nor an umbrella, and to show up drenched and bedraggled at the police station in the dead of night… wouldn't that in itself be suspicious? He wasn't even sure where the police station was.

The child woke to bright sunshine streaming in through a small window. He squinted and rubbed his eyes. Such a bright sun he had never seen; it didn't shine like this in his village. "Maybe in the next village it will be even brighter," he thought. He flung off the towel that covered him and sprang to his feet. "En garde!" With his mother he'd been reading a child's version of *The Three Musketeers*, and he had learned the French phrase. Unsheathing an imaginary sword, he leapt to the attack, but the ungainly attire he still wore – he'd fallen asleep without undressing – hampered his movements, and looked funny besides. He laughed. What had the old man done with his clothes? They should be dry by now – but no, there they lay in a heap on the floor, hardly less wet

214

than when he'd taken them off. He gathered them up and went outside. That sun would dry them in no time. Its brightness was still painful. His mother had told him about places far, far away where the sun was so hot you couldn't stand it unless you were born and grew up there. Could this be one of those places? Could he have come as far as that? Near the shed he'd been about to crawl into yesterday stood a giant tree with numerous branches. At home it would have been called an oak tree, but this one, though as large as an oak, was somehow different, he was not sure exactly how. Standing on tiptoes and stretching to the very limit of his strength, he managed, just barely, to reach the lowest branch, and to hang his clothes on it.

Were there any children about? Venturing forth, he looked around him as best he could. Even with eyes half shut he could not raise them much above ground level. His impression was of a village rather larger than his own. There were houses, stores and other buildings. They cast large shadows. They must be very tall. Retreating to the shade of the giant tree, he opened his eyes wide, but everything he saw seemed somehow mysterious and beyond his comprehension. He had been right about the buildings, they were very tall, almost frighteningly so. His mother had told him the story of Don Quixote battling the windmills; now he imagined himself, dressed no less comically than Don Quixote, charging the buildings as if they were giants. They *were* giants – but even odder than their size was the fact that there was not a soul in sight. His own village at this hour would be bustling with people going about their business. "Maybe the people here are invisible," he thought. He imagined the buildings, sidewalks and roads, deserted to his sun-dazzled eyes, swarming with invisible people – could they see him? Maybe they could, and were crowding around him, demanding to know who he was and what he was doing there, growing angry at his failure to answer, perhaps shouting at him and preparing to beat him. "I can't hear you!" he cried. Did they believe him? He waited, tensed against an assault that did not come – or maybe it had come; "maybe they're beating me now, only I can't feel it. En garde!" he shouted, and laughed. "If people here were invisible, then that funny old man would be too, wouldn't he?"

He was hungry, and wandered back to the house. In the garden he came upon the old man, digging a hole with a shovel.

"Are you burying somebody?" asked the child.

"I'll bury you," grumbled the old man. He had not slept all night and was bedraggled, disheveled and irritable.

"I'm hungry."

Paying no attention, the old man dumped the contents a paper bag into the hole and began covering it up.

"What's that?" the child asked.

"Fish bones."

"What are you burying fish bones for?"

"To make a fish tree."

"What?"

"From apple seeds come apple trees, right? From pear seeds, pear trees, right? Well, plant fish bones and you get a fish tree."

"You're joking, right?"

"Do I look like I'm joking?"

"No."

"Well, then."

"Is *that* a fish tree?" asked the child, pointing to the giant tree by the shed.

"I'm in no mood for joking. We have to get you back to your people. Today. Now. I can't be responsible for you. I'm too old, and you're too…"

"Young?"

"Too young – yes, too young!" he exploded, as though the child had said something intolerably provoking. "What did you come to me for? Why to me, of all the people in the world? Eh? Well? Answer!"

Not at all frightened or disconcerted, the child replied calmly, "I didn't come to you. I just came."

"Well, now you can just go. I wash my hands of you. Go! Get off my property!"

"Can I have something to eat first?"

"No!"

The child shrugged and sauntered off. The old man watched in silence as the child turned into the main road and grew smaller and smaller. Soon he was lost to view altogether.

The old man picked up his shovel as though to resume his digging, but instead stood lost in thought, staring vacantly in front of him, not even noticing when the shovel fell from his hands and landed on the ground with a thud. After a time he roused himself. Leaving the shovel where it lay he made his way to the shed he'd caught the child creeping into. He was stooping to go inside when he noticed, hanging from the lowest branch and swaying rather wildly in the stiffening breeze, the child's clothes. He paused in bewilderment. Had the child forgotten them? Left them there on purpose? Surely he wouldn't go far dressed as he was, in that white shirt

217

hanging down to his knees and belted with a tie? What kind of bizarre child was he, anyway? "Am I the only child in the world?" "My mummy said I come from heaven." No, that was no ordinary child. "And I chased him away, I let him go off alone and hungry; he'll die on the road, or be murdered, and here are his clothes, on my property, with my fingerprints all over them, evidence… evidence of what? Well, evidence. Evidence is evidence! Should I burn them? What good will that do? He's wearing my shirt, confound him!"

As day followed day and nothing happened, the old man began to wonder if the child had been a figment of his imagination. "Living alone like this unhinges a man, you get to the point where you can't tell fantasy from reality…" There were the clothes, of course – "why didn't I burn them? I will burn them." But he couldn't bring himself to do it, or even to approach the shed where he had tossed them after taking them down from the tree. *Had* he in fact tossed them there? Did they exist? He could settle the question once and for all by simply going to the shed and glancing inside. Either they were there or they were not. If they were, the child was real; if not, he was not. But a kind of terror seized him at the thought of pursuing the matter. He could not account for it. He was prey lately to all sorts of vague terrors. In his younger days he'd been afraid of nothing, had hardly known what fear was. Now he was afraid of everything.

"Well, I'll just forget it," he decided. "He's nothing to me. I wash my hands of him. I wash my hands! What's it to me whether he's real or not?"

The villagers all gathered in the square to greet their returning mayor. His tour abroad had been a triumph, and he was feted accordingly. The contracts he had secured would assure prosperity for generations to come. As the chairman of the welcoming committee put it in his speech, "You, sir, have put our village on the map!"

Fresh from the festivities, the mayor went home and got a surprise. His child had left home and had been missing for a day and a half before being found on a remote road and brought back.

"He thinks," said his wife, "that he's the only child in the world. He went off in search of other children."

The mayor frowned. "It's those stories you're always telling him."

"Stories?"

"Fairy tales, fantasies."

"Is it wrong to tell a child fairy tales?"

"Well, you see what they do to him! He's lost all sense of reality!"

"The reality, my dear, is that there are hardly any children around any more. When we were children it was different."

The mayor was thoughtful. "Yes," he said, softening his tone, "yes, that's true. Hm. Well, he'll start school in April. He'll get some of the nonsense knocked out of him there, I'm sure."

"You shouldn't have closed our school."

"*I* shouldn't have! Is it my fault? Didn't I do everything in my power to save it? It's not a fairy tale world, my dear. There are economic realities, political realities, demographic realities. You can't wish them away! When people have fewer children, enrollment falls; when enrollment falls, schools close. I think under the circumstances we made the best arrangements possible. Our local children will be bussed to the school in the next village – a perfectly good school, I know the headmaster personally."

"There's a man he met who put him up for the night. He gave him food and dry clothes – rather strange clothes" – she could not help laughing at the thought. "We must go and thank him."

"Hm. Is the bath ready?" Judging from where the boy was found, the man would not have been a local voter. The mayor's consequent lack of interest in him was instinctive rather than calculated, and his wife by now understood this well enough to sigh where once she might have remonstrated. "Foreign countries," said the mayor, "are all very well, but when it comes to bathing, we could teach them a thing or two, I think! Yes indeed!"

"There is no such thing, my little man, as a fish tree."

"There is!" the child insisted hotly. "I saw it."

Usually it was his mother who put him to bed, and he was a little surprised to see his father stride into the room instead. "Isn't mummy going to tell me a story?"

"I thought," said the mayor, "that you and I would have a little talk. About 'fish trees,' about 'the only child in the world'... You see, my boy, you'll be starting school soon, and it's time you learned that some things are real and some things are not. And those things that are not you must put out of your mind. Because in school, you see – "

"The fish tree is real! The old man grows fish trees with fish bones. There was this tree, this huge tree; I said, 'What kind of tree is it?' and he said" – deepening his voice to a comic imitation of geriatric hoarseness – 'It's a fish tree, my little man.'"

The child's father smiled. "Did he really say, 'My little man'?"

The child reddened. That was his father's pet name for him, and he'd stupidly put it in the old man's mouth. His father would think he was making it up. How would he ever convince him now?

"And what's this about being the only child in the world? Eh?"

The child lowered his eyes and said nothing.

"There are children all over the place. I can name every child in this village. Can you?"

The mayor waited. Still the child did not speak.

"I thought not. How do you think it looks to my constituents when my own child refuses to play with other children? Eh?"

"They're stupid."

"All of them?" But the mayor hesitated to insist. It was true. They certainly were less bright than his own son.

"You're sleepy now." The mayor stood up. "You think over what I've said. We'll talk again in the morning. Or rather... no, first thing tomorrow morning I'm giving a speech at the Chamber of Commerce." He bent down and kissed the boy lightly on the forehead. "Goodnight, little man. Oh, and see here. No more wandering off like that, eh? – without a word to your mother, leaving her to worry. Understood?"

All this, of course, happened a very long time ago. The mayor was returned to office again and again; he died in office and his son took over; the son governs to this day and is himself getting on in years; he has hinted more than once at retirement, but the people will not hear of it; they gather in the streets in such numbers to demand he carry on that he yields, fearing chaos if he does not. These are unstable times. The village became a town under his father's government, and a city under his; many of the surrounding villages, including that of the fish tree, once the bigger of the two, have been incorporated into it. The mayor's mother is still alive. She is very old but still hale and healthy. Rather than move in with the mayor and his family, as he has repeatedly urged her to do, she insists on living alone and independently. Rumor has it that she is not as proud of her son as his achievements and his popular adulation would entitle her to be; there are those who say she nurses even now a secret sorrow at seeing the boy take so thoroughly after his father. But people will say anything about public figures who capture their imagination. The mayor has spoken of legislation to make the spread of falsehood a punishable criminal offense. He says only enemies of truth would oppose him. His opponents argue that you can't kill falsehood without killing truth as well. The mayor retorts that that is patent nonsense, and the public is largely on his side.

(2012)

222

CPSIA information can be obtained at www.ICGtesting.com
Printed in the USA
BVOW06s0044030316

438761BV00009B/166/P

9 781621 377658